HUMOUR
THERAPY

BRANKO BOKUN

HUMOUR THERAPY

in
cancer, psychosomatic diseases,
mental disorders, crime, interpersonal
and sexual relationships

VITA BOOKS
26 Chelsea Square, London SW3

© Branko Bokun 1986

No parts of this book may be reproduced without permission from the publisher, except for quotation of brief passages in criticism.

ISBN 0-9510525-0-0

1. Anthropology 2. Medicine
3. Philosophy   4. Psychiatry
        5. Sociology

First edition — January 1986
Second edition — October 1986

Published by Vita Books,
26 Chelsea Square, London SW3

Printed by VERITAS FOUNDATION PRESS
4-12 Praed Mews, London W2 1QZ. England
Type-set by "UNICORN" Publishing Studio
132, Dorchester Waye, Hayes, Middx. UB4 0HZ
Great Britain

My grateful thanks to
Anne Loudon for her help
in writing this book.

CONTENTS

Part I

Introduction	11
Amusement and laughter	35
Humour	43
Mature way of reasoning	49
Emotion, memory and a sense of humour	53
Humour as medicine	73
Humour and mental disorders	85
Humour and pregnancy	99
Humour and sexual deviations	103
Crime, punishment and humour	109
Leisure	113
Humour as our only saviour	117
Courses in a sense of humour	121

Part II

Self-importance	135
Self-realisation	139
Religion	141
'The sad reality'	145
Eastern escapism	147
Escape into the past	151
Revolution	155
Science and technology	159
Economy and the Welfare State	163
Aggression	183
Loneliness	193
Interpersonal relationships	199
Sexual relationships	207

First edition — January 1986
Second edition — October 1986

ERRATA

Page:	Line:	It reads:	It should read:
40	3 t	In	If
41	7 b	tough	laugh
74	4 b	focus	locus
149	7 t	o	of
179	15 t	thought	taught
195	7 t	owns	one's

t — from the top of the page.
b — from the bottom of the page.

PART I

PART 1

INTRODUCTION

Before starting my theory on humour and its therapeutic potential, I feel it would help to try and appraise the origin of our species, its evolution, the development of our mind, and of our present way of reasoning and behaving.

'From some kind of Miocene Ape, probably living in Africa, both apes and men are descended. The apes' ancestors, after a trial period on the ground, swung back into the trees. Ours stayed below, rose onto their hind legs, made tools, walked, talked and became hunters'. Most students of human evolution would not question this explanation of Carlton S. Coon in his 'History of Man'.

Presumably Mr. Coon was having us on. What animal would ever willingly leave an ideal environment for an inferno? Our forefathers knew how dangerous life was on the ground, which was why they had originally fled up into the tree-tops. Apart from other perils, malevolent and poisonous snakes lay in wait on the ground. Even today, the mere sight of snakes triggers off flight or hysterics in primates and humans.

Fear of falling from the safety of trees could explain why many people still today are jolted awake from a nightmare of falling.

Bearing in mind that the human brain only started expanding fast about a million years ago, and only became capable of abstract thought, and so of absurdities, relatively recently, surely our ancestors would never have been so absurd as to leave an ideal environment for such danger.

In those days the human species were less than three feet tall, and with a brain less than a third the size of today's gorilla.

What could have actually happened?

There is strong evidence that the climate deteriorated dramatically during the Miocene period, between twenty-six and thirteen million years ago, replacing much of the woodlands with vast stretches of savannah. The first creatures to be driven from a restricted area would surely be the least competitive, the weakest, the least developed and the least aggressive.

It is logical, therefore, to assume that man is neither the offspring of fallen angels, nor of elevated apes; man springs from fallen apes. The bible is more accurate than the anthropologists in its explanation of the origin of man. Our ancestors, our Adams and Eves were indeed evicted from Paradise. Not by Almighty God, however, but by fitter apes.

Even today there are signs that prove man's lack of development. For example his body is less symmetric, particularly regarding the efficiency of his arms and legs, compared with the bodies of other primates. We are either right-handed (90% approx.), or left-handed (10% approx.). In reality this means a defficiency in the dexterity of the left hand for the right-handed, and vice-versa. The efficiency of the paws and claws of other primates is more or less equally distributed. Our brain is also highly assymetric. Many people may suggest that due to this assymetry we became more advanced in the ability of thinking than other primates. But, we are also more advanced in the sinister way of thinking.

The evolution of our species and the appearance of Homo sapiens may be better understood if we start from the premise that our ancestors, and particularly our male ancestors, were physiologically less developed and less mature than the ancestors of other primates.

A lack of maturity, aggressiveness and specialisation were perhaps an advantage in the new environment, since to be able to improve one has to be open to changes, to be vulnerable. Animals, such as crocodiles, which were perfectly adapted two hundred million years ago have hardly evolved since. If we had been better developed, we would never have needed to invent tools; if we were by nature aggressive, as many insist we are, nature would have given us an innate instrument of aggression, and we would not have needed to invent all kinds of weapons. Without the disadvantage of the body's hairlessness, we would never have had to invent clothing.

I also feel that if our ancestors had voluntarily left the woodlands, we would never have developed nostalgia and dreams about this 'green and pleasant land', this myth of a lost paradise. Political Utopias which promise a life of abundance, safety and happiness, a life of bliss in which playing is the main activity, the life that we lost in the woodlands, could only be inspired by nostalgia.

Even today, most scientists agree that we are in a phase of infancy or neotany. 'The characteristic which is so vital for the human peculiarity of the true man, that of always remaining in a state of development, is quite certainly a gift we owe to the neotaneous nature of mankind', writes K. Lorenz.

Why? What is the main characteristic of neoteny or infancy?

The answer is simply play.

Play is a random, flexible and exploratory activity. Play increases experience and understanding, and this was and still is of major importance to a species without a strong innate pattern of behaviour.

Exploratory play, this experimental activity, was what our ancestors relied on to discover how best to adapt to the new environment and conditions. Play became our ancestors' main tool of survival, their only specialisation. Man was helped in inventing useful instruments by play. Tools could have been invented from toys. Homo ludens preceded Homo faber.

It could be questioned that if we are a neotenous species, therefore playful and joyful by nature, why so many people, and much of the time, are in a state of lugubrious seriousness or gloom? What was it that transformed a happy, giggling, pleasant and innocuous species into a discontented, often depressive, and aggressive lot?

If we were an infantile or neotenous species it is natural to assume that we were guided and ruled by our mothers. Most women acquire a natural maturity with motherhood, a common sense mentality and the instinct to protect, share and care.

There is, in fact, a certain evidence that for millions of years, the human communities were guided and ruled by women. The first supreme divinities the world over were mother-goddesses.

For example, one of the oldest known statuettes, 'Venus of Laussel', dating from around 27,000 years ago, represents a powerful woman. A woman's torso, 25,000 years old, was found in Ostrva Petrovice in Czechoslovakia. Another impressive statuette of a woman, 18,000 years old, was found in Willendorf in Austria.

In Egypt, the goddess Isis was the wife and saver of Osiris, the supreme god of the Underworld, and mother of the living god, Horus.

In Minoan Crete, there was the mother-goddess culture and civilization. Woman's high position in Ancient Crete can be deduced from the artistic remains found in Knossos.

In China, during the Shang dynasty (1766-1123 B.C.) and during the Chou dynasty (1123-256 B.C.) life was dominated by Shen nu, 'the divine woman'.

In Homer's Greece, the women and female divinities, apart from Athena who had no mother, just a father, worked consciously while the men and male gods played war games, tricks or practical jokes, crying like children whenever something went wrong.

By the VI Century B.C., however, Greece achieved male supremacy. Women became the main characters in Greek tragedies.

With Judeo-Christianity, the total dominance of men became established and the subordination of women was institutionalised.

How did this wise and protective mother's style of reasoning and guidance, which helped the human species to survive for so many millions of years get destroyed? What was responsible for changing the inoffensive groups of food gatherers into hordes of violent and unscrupulous killers?

The answer must be the adolescent male.

Our species have always had a longer adolescence than other primates, and more pronounced in males than females.

The adolescent phase is the stage in which an individual emerges from infancy with its obedience, imitation and dependence on the mother and on the group, but has not yet reached maturity or settled inside the community.

Adolescence is generally a state of awkwardness and clumsiness, which perhaps disturbed the established order, and irritated the rest of the community. Sooner or later, however, the reaction of the group cooled down most of the rebellious adolescents, giving them their place and rank in the community. But, those individuals who could not integrate or refused to adapt themselves to the established order of the group, those who continued to persevere in their adolescent mentality and behaviour, were ignored or abandoned.

These lonely rejected adolescents, living on the edge of the communities, started forming gangs, creating a radical change in the life of the human species. With their 'adolescent revolutions', they replaced the natural order based on mother-infant relationships, with their own. These adolescent revolutions took place between twelve and two thousand years ago. By the end of the fourth millenium, B.C., in the Vinca area of Central Serbia, and the Sesklo area in Northern Greece, evidence of the change was unearthed. Figurines of male nudes, proudly holding their penises were already in prominence.

With the adolescent revolutions, the history of humanity became a chain of revolutions engineered by the adolescent mentality in search of stability, a difficult goal to reach, as adolescence implies restlessness and rebellion.

Ever since that era started, humanity has been ruled by gangs, gangs formed by lonely adolescent-minded individuals.

Where and how did these adolescents find the audacity to challenge the established order which had cared for our species for so long? Where and how did they find their aggression and the temerity to use force against the natural laws and rules? Above all, where and how did these adolescents find the energy to feed their audacity, their aggression and their violence?

In order to answer these questions, I would like to insert an important point.

Life consists of bioenergy which is provided by instability and fears which are characteristic of organic matter.

Like any other species, we are born with a certain range of basic life-energy associated with a certain range of basic innate fears, characteristic of a species. Being provided by fears, our bioenergy can be increased above its normal range, provided by our basic inherited fears, mainly by acquiring extra fears.

Without the care and protection of his community, the isolated adolescent developed extra fears, the fears that loneliness produces, terrible fears for an individual born to live as a social animal.

Because of these fears, the isolated individual developed self-awareness with its defensive mechanism of selfishness and self-centredness. This pushed him even deeper into isolation and loneliness.

The first consequence of these new fears was the decreasing efficiency of our rejected ancestors' sensory and perceptive systems. These extra fears created by loneliness, produced new emotional arousals which led to the distortion of our senses and perceptions.

An even more significant consequence of the increased emotional arousals was a marked change in the activity of the brain.

Our brain's mental activity is stimulated, ruled and provided with energy by emotional arousals. Even the slightest difference in emotional arousals can create different conditions of our brain, a difference in its mental activity. What is more, the brain is also a gland and its glandular activity can be manipulated by thoughts or ideas created by the brain's mental activity.

In his loneliness, the adolescent's undeveloped innate patterns of behaviour became confused, creating doubt and hesitation. This opened the way to the speculative activity of his brain.

For millions of years, the life of the community was based on natural order. Without this order, an isolated and lonely individual developed a craving for it. This craving is still with us.

This isolated adolescent, therefore, acquired the following: reduced efficiency of sense-perception, an activity of the brain on higher emotional levels, hesitation, and a search for order.

These four new acquisitions produced a new cognitive mechanism: the mind with its world of approximations, assumptions, opinions, beliefs, hopes, hypotheses and fantasies.

When isolated from its group, any social animal, especially in its adolescence, develops extra fears, high emotional arousals which confuse its sensory and perceptive systems, pushing its brain towards some kind of fantasies which are reflected in its unnatural behaviour.

Our mind, therefore, is a result of our brain's activity in a state of higher emotional arousals produced by inquietude, uncertainity and fears of an isolated and lonely individual.

Individuals living in communities, and particularly in communities influenced or ruled by mothers, fantasise far less than those living in societies cultivating individual independence. Prophets of all times withdrew to the wilderness in order to increase the activity of their minds. Emotional arousals increased by fears of loneliness in the wilderness can inhibit the sense-perception to the point of enabling hermits to have apparitions, revelations or visions. Distortions of the sense-perception by drugs or alcohol result in all kinds of aberrations or hallucinations.

From the beginning of its existence, the mind created its powerful weapon of self-assertion: faith. The mind invented faith because only faith can bring hope to a world of beliefs.

Hope could only have been invented by a brain working with distorted perceptions. A distorted perception allows for guessing, and speculation, and guessing and speculation are guided by an inner longing to reduce or to placate feelings of vulnerability. The brain's speculations, inspired by the longing to reduce or to placate feelings of vulnerability and fears, has created our characteristic, unique to the adolescent humanity: that of wishful thinking.

The Ancient Greeks knew that the mind was a creation of wishfulness: they placed it in their chests. The Latins placed it 'in pectore'. The Ancient Egyptians located the seat of their minds in their hearts. 'I planned in my heart how I should make every shape'. Atun-Re explains, following a Heliopolis myth.

How did this adolescent wishful-thinking solve the problem of the discomfort caused by the fears he had acquired as an isolated and lonely individual?

The adolescent mind found the easiest solution: escape. It started escaping from reality into its world of imagination and fantasies.

The idea of escape from reality into a world of fantasy may have been inspired in the neo-cortex by the first of the following three innate ways used by our old brain to solve discomfort: flight, fight or hide. Between the old brain and cerebral cortex, there is a rich bilateral neuronal inter-connection which could have allowed the latter to be influenced in its imaginative activity and ideas by the natural responses of the former.

In his fantasy, the adolescent replaced his inadequate and fragile self with an idea of self, an idealised 'ought to be' self.

In the above mentioned Egyptian myth, Atun-Re 'came into being of himself'.

When the adolescent invented his idealised self, he became infatuated by it. It is in the nature of a creator to fall in love with his creation.

With self-love, the adolescent's 'I' became the centre of the Universe. Perhaps that is why humanity took so long to discover a Copernicus. In the English Language, 'I' is still a capital letter.

With the appearance of the mind, our sense-perception became even more distorted. Today people with fanatical political or religious beliefs can reach total insensitivity and insensibility.

With the appearance of the mind, the brain's common sense reasoning and intelligence activity was replaced by the mind's wishful thinking guided by the interest and logic of the pretentious self-invented ego.

We all know that those who lean on their mind's prejudices or beliefs are unable to use their common sense reasoning or behave in accordance with it. 'Not our logical, measurative faculty, but our imaginative one is king over us,' Stressed Carlyle in his 'Sartor Resartus'.

Frequently we do not care about our reduced sensitivity and sensibility imposed by the activity of the mind, as the inaccuracy and distortion of our perceiving apparatus and intellect help us in our fantasies and daydreaming.

At this point one could ask why, if humans enjoy living in their imaginary world of the mind, are they not more joyful and happier?

During adolescence we start taking the world of the mind too seriously, and develop confidence in our wishful ideas. From time to time children and mature men and women also develop certain fantasies, but they merely play with them, even if sometimes they seem to take them seriously.

Taking the world of the mind too seriously, created an abstract seriousness which I shall call over-seriousness, as it is in the nature of abstractions to exaggerate: with exaggeration they hope to become reality. In this craving I find the origin of human aggression. Abstractions can only become reality by fighting reality, by forcing it to suit the world of the mind.

By taking his mind over-seriously, the adolescent's natural vivacious, cheerful and flexible face and body changed, reflecting the tension of over-seriousness. Many of the hard lines or distortions on a face are carved by a stubborn belief, a fixed idea or an arrogant prejudice.

How can wishful thinking and the fantasies of the mind create tension? How can the mind's prejudices and beliefs create the necessary energy for their aggression and realisation?

By escaping from frightening reality into the world of the mind, we develop yet another new fear, that brooding fear of the failure of our wishful expectations and hopes. We develop a dread that our pretentions may not materialise.

Sooner or later we sense the discrepancy between our mind's idealised ego, and the abilities of our true self to realise its pretentions. Sensing the precariousness and vulnerability of our abstract existence, we develop the fear that our inflated ego might be a loser.

The awareness of these mind's created fears, like the awareness of any real fear, communicated to the brain by our senses, triggers off a state of alarm or emergency.

In order to make my theories clearer, I would like to insert an important explanation here.

The main regulator of our internal energy is the autonomic nervous system. This is composed of the parasympathetic and sympathetic systems. Being in charge of our organism's constructive metabolism, of the secretion of the juices in our alimentary canals necessary for the digestion of food, and of the excretion of superfluous material from our body, the parasympathetic system aims to realise a relatively stable physiological well-being, a resting state.

Sudden and exceptional circumstances, particulary those threatening our survival, trigger off the activity of the sympathetic system. The purpose of this is to create extra energy in our body to enable it to cope with an emergency, mainly to fight or flee the danger. The symphatetic system is in charge of the destructive metabolism involving the release of energy.

It is important to stress that any excessive increase in the activity of the sympathetic system reduces the activity of the parasympathetic system which upsets the normal body's functioning, thereby shaking our biological welfare.

Fear for the survival of our imaginary ego is the main instigator of the extra energy in our body, and, at the same time, is the main enemy of our physiological well-being. Usually we are more worried about the survival of our ideal ego than the survival of our true self.

Most of our absurd, unnecessary or irrational activities, of our restlessness and agitation, our avidity and envy, are backed by the energy provided by the fears of our mind, fears that our ambitions, wishfulness and expectations may not be fulfilled, fears of the failure of our hopes, or the dread of losing that which our mind considers its positive achievements.

These mind's created fears stimulate our hypothalamus. The hypothalamus, which controls our autonomic nervous system, triggers off the activity of the sympathetic system, and through the pituitary gland, activates the secretion of the adrenaline and noradrenaline.

Through the pituitary gland, our hypothalamus can also activate the thyroid gland which increases the rate of oxidative processes and metabolism, improving the body's state of energy.

Released by the activated sympathetic system, the neurotransmitters accelerate the heartbeat and increase the blood pressure.

Adrenaline increases the oxygen consumption at the tissue level, stimulates the heart, increasing cardiac output, and raises the level of energy providing glucose in the blood, thereby improving the tonus of the voluntary muscles, creating readiness for action.

Noradrenaline re-inforces the blood pressure by narrowing the peripheral blood vessels and small arteries. It also widens the arterioles of the voluntary muscles, essential for a quick and decisive reaction.

The neurotransmitters of the symapthetic nervous system and the hormones of the adrenal and thyroid glands, therefore, mobilise a chain of the body's cells, imposing extra activity on them. Nature provides this mechanism to create extra energy and readiness to enable an individual to solve the problem of a sudden temporary alarm or emergency, through the philogenetically programmed drives of fight or flight.

With its persistent wishful ideas and its perserving prejudices or beliefs, our mind, however, creates a lasting precariousness and a protracted fear of defeat. (Self-love, self-infatuation, wishful thoughts and beliefs are constantly under threat in the mind of the beholder).

The lasting precariousness of our mind's world and the protracted fear of defeat of our self-created self can produce a more or less permanent state of alarm which results in a more or less permanent emotional arousal. Not being discharged in flight or fight, the arousal becomes a biological discomfort, an inner irritation, stress or tension.

I shall call this typically human arousal, caused by overserious abstractions, the psychosomatic, or mind created emotional arousal to distinguish it from a natural arousal. Natural arousal is mainly caused by an automatic reaction of the sympathetic system and adrenal glands to real danger perceived by the senses. This reaction is usually of a temporary nature as the problem is quickly solved, by both animal and man, with fight, flight or hiding. The solution of the problem eliminates the extra activity of the sympathetic system, thus allowing a fuller activity of the parasympathetic system which returns the body to a better physical well-being and a healthier physiological existence and activity.

Psychosomatic emotional arousal, instead, is produced by the mind, and remains alive in the body all the time the mind is active.

We rarely discharge our arousal by fighting or by fleeing the world of the mind which caused it. Even more seldom do we hide from the world of our mind in order to placate the fear which caused the arousal. We have therefore reached a new phenomenon in nature: we are able to have a permanently strained organism serving our capricious and pretentious mind.

Our psychosomatic emotional arousal is the price we pay for

living in a world of imagination and fantasy, by living dangerously in the uncertain world of the mind created by daydreaming or wishful thinking.

The wider the discrepancy between our pretentions and our ability to reach them, the bigger our mind's created arousal. This arousal can be increased by either increasing our pretentions, or by decreasing our abilities. We can increase our pretentiousness by acquiring new political or economic rights, by a higher standard of living, by cultural, technological or scientific achievements, or by magnifying our self-infatuation and self-importance.

Our ability and potential can diminish with ill-health, tiredness, invalidness, political and economic restrictions, a hostile new environment, being a minority in a collectivity, and by losing a loved one.

Causing a biological discomfort, and inner irritation or stress, this psychosomatic arousal craves discharge.

In this psychosomatic arousal, created by the sense of precariousness or vulnerability of the mind's world, and its craving for discharge, these lonely adolescents found their audacity, aggressiveness, strength and energy to challenge and eliminate the established natural order, dominated by the mother-infant relationship.

In this psychosomatic emotional arousal, the human mind found its power to will, and this inspired the supreme aim of the adolescent mentality: the will for power.

That this extra energy is acquired with the development of the mind and its fears, can be deduced by the fact that when parts of our brain, mainly its frontal lobes where the activity of the mind seems to take place, are damaged or removed, we lose a great deal of this extra energy.

United by certain abstract ideas or beliefs, these rootless adolescents formed gangs and imposed their way of thinking, believing and behaving onto the social groups. The mature women and men gradually adapted to the new style of life. Their common-sense intelligence and experience became intimidated by the arrogance and aggressiveness of the new mentality. Some women, particularly the young and single, even started to adopt the new way of thinking and behaving, thus acquiring the male adolescent mentality, some becoming even more arrogant and aggressive than the men.

With the adolescent revolution, a life began in which the irrational mind inhibited or eliminated rational intellect. Backed by its psychosomatic arousal, therefore by audacity, arrogance and aggressiveness, the irrational easily imposed itself on the inoffensive and peace-loving rational. Absurdities, incongruities, the paranormal and paradoxes became a normal part of life.

With the adolescent revolution, humanity started reconciling two incompatibilities: man's longing to belong, and his selfishness. Belonging meant dependence, and dependence meant the degradation of the adolescent's acquired individual independence. The adolescent minded tried, and still try, to organise social life around their selfishness, self-centredness and the cult of individuality. They succeeded in replacing the naturally formed communities, based on mutual dependence and help, with systems of societies based on the association of isolated individuals. The life of any system of society organised by selfish individuals, became a life of mutual exploitation.

The gangs imposed their mentality and their style of life with violence, terror and murder, previously unknown to the human species. The first male divinity, Marduk, in order to become the omnipotent god of the Sumerian pantheon, killed his mother. The myth of the origin of Rome, in which a gang of alienated adolescents raided Sabine and enslaved the peaceful neighbouring villages, also depicts the new mentality. The gang in power introduced a novelty: armies. Their task was not to protect the gang against unaggressive rational maturity, but against other adolescent gangs with opposing ideas or beliefs.

Humanity began devoting a great deal of energy and resourses to armament. The world today spends around two and a half million dollars on weapons every minute. During the same time, at least thirty people die of starvation.

The adolescent mentality eliminated the natural family group formed around the 'mater-familias'. Man replaced this form of family with what he considered the ideal family, a family dominated by a wishful idea invented by his mind: the 'pater familias'.

Man then created an even more absurd situation by imposing respect and even worship of his new ideas by the use of force and violence. Moral and religious codes and social laws were introduced. This novelty in nature brought another novelty: the police, created in order to enforce these artificially made codes and laws.

With the adolescent revolution, man changed another basic law of nature: he replaced the female's initiative in sexual relations. Sexual exploits became an important booster to his ego. The cult of the bull, this symbol of sexual vigour and potency, was born.

When man realised the difficulties of keeping his woman, or women under his spell with his virility, he invented a new idea: marriage and fidelity. Woman's infidelity and adultery were a grave offence to man's self-inflated ego, and were punished by death.

If man was naturally superior to woman, many of woman's duties and obligations would have never become legally binding.

Men became Narcisists. Man saw himself with his sixth sense, with his mind.

The new mentality developed a phobia about death. The thought of total annihilation mortified the adolescent's self-inflated ego. His mind, however, tried and still tries, to placate this fear of death by inventing the immortal soul, eternal life after death, and even re-incarnation.

There is evidence that fears can stimulate the secretion of the brain's opiates, known as endophins and enkephalins, for a certain amount of time. These opiates are similar in their chemical composition and their effects to the opiate morphine.

Scientists explain that the secretion of these natural opiates is originated by stress. In my opinion, the secretion just coincides with stress, because the secretion of the brain's opiates and stress have the same origin: fears.

The brain's opiates, also called natural pain-killers, do not alleviate or eliminate stress. They only reduce the physically painful side of it, and this can be negative as the function of pain is that of an early warning system, calling for the intervention and repair of body damage. These opiates may have a certain value in reducing the physical pain of the deadly bites of predators, of placating the pain of those mortally wounded in war, or in helping to face mortal accidents. Inhibiting the functions of pain as an early warning system in ordinary life, however, these natural opiates can be dangerous as they bring many people to an abrupt collapse or sudden unexpected death, caused by stress.

In the same way as naturally provoked emergencies or dangers, the mind's created fears also trigger off the brain's secretion of its opiates. Sensing this, some people produce fears or worries in their minds in order to escape from reality into self-induced drug-like states of existence. Enjoying their drug-like states of existence, these people keep changing their fears or worries. Consciously or unconsciously, they do this because they realise that in persevering with the same ones, the secretion of the brain's opiates and their effect are gradually reduced, then eliminated. Most of the time, these fears and worries are mere trivialities, over-dramatised in the mind.

The tendency to enjoy worries is exploited by the media which emphasises bad news.

Massochists do not enjoy the actual ill-treatment, but the drug-like moments realised by the brain's opiates, the secretion of which is stimulated by the humiliation of their egos by the ill-treatment.

The pleasure of self-flagellation is also caused by the brain's opiates, whose release is triggered off by 'a soul in pain' or an ego's mortification, created by the self-flagellation.

The working of the natural opiates, the duration of their effects and the reaction after these effects have worn off, is best illustrated in near death accidents. Those who have been through a serious accident have usually experienced euphoric bliss immediately preceeding the accident. Soon after, when the effect of the natural opiates have vanished, the lucky survivors start feeling the physical pain of the injuries, or they enter a trembling or panicky state.

With the adolescent mentality, another curious phenomenon occured: suffering of the mind. The mind suffers whenever its conceited ego is threatened, offended or hurt. Buddha was wrong to attribute the causes of human suffering to ignorance; he would have done better had he attributed them to conceit and pretentiousness which only start when ignorance disappears, when we think we know better.

Sufferings of the mind stimulate the extra activities of the sympathetic nervous system and of the adrenal glands, and this produces tension and stress, characteristic of an alarming state of existence.

Many people call the adrenal glands' secreted substances 'stress hormones', as they are supposed to help us fight stress. In my view, it is the presence of an extra quantity of these hormones and of the neuro-transmitters of the sympathetic nervous system, which create emotional arousals, therefore anxiety, tension and stress. In fact a state of anxiety, tension and stress is realised if we are injected with an extra dose of adrenaline.

The mind's created emotional arousals produce sensations of tension, anxiety and stress mainly because of the spasm of the smooth muscles caused by the presence in our body of an extra quantity of adrenal hormones and the neuro-transmitters of the sympathetic nervous system.

Sufferings of the mind brought a significant change in the field of physical pain.

Opiates produced by the mind's fears, worries or sufferings, can create partial or even total insensivity to physical pain while they are secreted and remain effective.

Prolonged fears, worries or sufferings of the mind, however, progressively reduce and eliminate both the secretion of these opiates, and their analgesic effect. After the effect of the opiates has gone, the physical pain often becomes intolerable.

Why do those with prolonged fears, worries or sufferings of the mind feel physical pain more deeply than those without?

In my view, the answer is that the tensity, stiffness or rigidity of the body, due to the spasm of the muscles, produced by the minds fears, worries or sufferings increase the intensity of the physical pain by stressing, pressing or irritating the damaged parts of the body.

People with highly inflated egos are offended by physical pain, which increases the frustration and sufferings of the mind. After the initial short insouciance, due to the effect of the natural opiates, the prolonged frustration and sufferings of the mind can increase the physical pain of those offended by it, to agony.

That the mind's suffering increases physical pain can be deduced by the fact that when the front lobes, where the activity of the mind and its suffering seem to take place, of those with a chronic physical pain, are eliminated or cut off from the rest of the brain, they feel less physical pain, presumably because they are less worried either by it, or about their egos.

Mobilising the activities of the sympathetic nervous system and adrenal glands, the adolescent mind's lasting worries and sufferings reduce the efficiency of the body's immune and self-repairing systems, thereby inhibiting the body's healing of the cause of the physical pain.

The physical wounds of those with inflated minds usually take longer to heal than the wounds of those who are less conceited. People with a sense of humour, small children and animals recover much better and quicker from injuries or surgery than humanity ruled by the self-precious adolescent mentality.

Being less inclined to self-infatuation and the mind's sufferings, most women bear physical pain and recover from it, better than men. On the other hand, women who develop self-opionated egos, become hysterical even when affected by a trivial bruise.

In cases in which our ego is seriously shaken in its very existence, like being abandoned by a loved one, or frustrated or offended in its infatuation, after a possible temporary euphoria, due to the release of the brain's opiates, the excessive and lasting activities of the sympathetic nervous system and adrenal glands can cause a chronic physical pain, a genuine disease, and sometimes an incurable illness.

Our ego is often seriously hurt by the success of others, mainly our relations or neighbours. In this case our mind's suffering may take the form of envy, and this can poison our existence.

With the start of the adolescent mentality, the human species became more accident prone than any other.

Apart from wanting to show-off, to prove their prowess, as in games or handling fast complicated machinery, self-infatuation reduces sensory alertness and increases the body's rigidity. These are the main causes of wounds, burns, broken bones etc...

The adolescent mentality also invented its own love. The love of an egoist can only be a selfish and exploiting love, a love of being loved. In this love, the lonely adolescent tried and still tries to find fulfillment.

The adolescent started falling in love with anything and anyone that boosted his ego, or aided his pretentiousness. Some women gradually adapted themselves to this originality in nature.

Placing his psychosomatic emotional arousals at the service of his desires, the adolescent initiated yet another novelty; passion. Passions soon became an escape from fears of inferiority, anonimity and banality. Increasing fear, this escape brings torments which often find their discharge in vindictive fits of passion. Political passions usually find their outlets in fanatical militancy.

Some of those obsessed by a passion often fall in love with their torments as these give them an illusion of living more importantly or more intensively.

We tend to explain that a passionate individual is obsessed by the object of his passion. In reality, this obsession is a consequence of his obsession for his selfish and narcisistic ego.

The absurd and comic nature of passions can be deduced by their aspirations. These are: material possession of etheral idealisations, a palpable seduction of a chimaera, a corporal union with a mirage.

There is another even more comic side of passions. As they imply discontent or the despise of an individual's real self, strong passions can inhibit his self-preservation. As they also diminish sexual interest and potency, intense passions could reduce interest in the preservation of the species.

The adolescent developed a yearning for possessions. He wanted to possess the persons and things with which he fell in love. With possessions, he hoped to compensate for his lack of belonging, for his loneliness.

These lonely and rootless individuals, born to live in a community, and longing to belong, found a unique solution to their unhappiness: they created an intimate relationship, intercourse with their belongings. They started belonging to their belongings, which transformed them into slaves of their possessions. It was not private property which alienated individuals, as Marx thought, it was alienated individuals who invented private property and personal wealth. People with the adolescent mentality will always be alienated in Capitalist, Communist, or any other system of society.

The adolescent mentality developed ideas of value, esteem and importance. The word value comes from the Latin 'valere', which in Ancient Rome, meant to rate or scale someone's wealth. The word esteem comes from the Latin 'aestimare', which originally meant to calculate or appraise someone's means or assets. The word importance comes from the Latin 'importare' which meant to bring valuables from the outside world into personal possession, to store goods safely at home. The idea of preciousness, stemming from the Latin word 'pretium', meaning price, was born.

The adolescent brought avidity, agitation and restlessness. The more self-infatuated he became, the more important his overblown ego felt, therefore the greedier, more agitated and restless he became.

The Western European conquest of the rest of the world was not due to Western European intelligence, but to its exceptional avidity, agitation and restlessness, all caused and inspired by the exceptional conceit and exaggerated cult of individualism which started with the Renaissance.

The new era replaced the innate co-operation among the members of a social species, with competition.

Competitiveness started with the mind's created fears or vulnerabilities. It is a result of restlessness or agitation, produced by the high adrenalin of emotional arousals caused by the fears or vulnerabilities of an adolescent inflated ego.

Perhaps the adolescent mentality became attracted by competition because in competition there had to be losers and victims, much needed by a fragile and insecure mind in search of self-assertion.

What the adolescent mentality never realised was that both success and victory isolated an individual even more, because the successful and the victorious are feared. To be feared, however, became a major aspiration of many of those ruled by the adolescent mentality.

The idea of competition and individual rivalry inspired the introduction of all kinds of games. In fact, life organised by the adolescent mentality was mainly centered around games, and the roles that games imply. Sports became glorified by the Greeks, which coincided with the glorification of the cult of the individual and his performance.

Play is recreative, while most games are unhealthy. Play is a joyful and salubrious physical and mental excercise, while most games are tense and strenuous. This is due to the fact that games involve antagonism and fight.

One can see the unhealthiness of games by explaining the origin of the extra energy needed by them.

As I have stressed, extra energy is generated by extra fears. The mind's fears of a bad performance, or losing a game, creates this extra energy. These mind's fears create a state of emergency and this increases the activities of the sympathetic nervous system and the adrenal glands, producing the extra energy necessary to fight or to win in a game. In nature, fighting is always triggered of by fears.

Following or watching sport, whether live or on the media, requires extra energy too. This is created by our enthusiasm, sometimes passion for one side or the other, developing fears that we are supporting the loser, therefore losing face. The emotional arousal created by this fear turns into heated agitation, which we call excitement.

The worry of losing stimulates the secretion of natural opiates, which often takes keen athletes to euphoria. Like drug addicts unable to get a 'fix', athletes can also have withdrawal symptoms when prevented from competing.

Blood samples taken from players at the end of a game, show high levels of adrenaline hormones and naturally produced opiates, and this is mainly reached by alarming or fearful states of existence.

Very competitive games can also be unhealthy because high levels of adrenaline and brain-produced opiates in the body can inhibit not only the individual's immune and self-repairing systems, but also the reproductive organs. During intensive training for major events, athletes often suffer temporary infertility. Recent research has shown that female athletes develop abnormal menstrual cycles, and male athletes a noticeable reduction in their testicular activity, diminishing the sperm count.

Perhaps Aristotle knew this when he advised that youngsters before puberty should only practice 'moderate games'.

The adolescent-minded tend to discharge their emotional arousals created by the fears of uncertainty into the search for success. Increasing pretentiousness or over-ambition, however, success increases the yearning for further success, which results in an even more frightening loneliness.

The adolescent minded also invented prayer. They started praying to supernatural forces to help their pretentions. The energy needed for prayer was, and still is, provided by the fear that our hopes or expectations may not be fulfilled. Many practice praying on their knees. The pious genuflection may have been inspired by the fact that the strong mind's fears twist the body, bending it at its hips and knees.

We are seldom surprised to see people praying in a church facing Christ dead on a cross. We would laugh, however, if we saw a group of sardines praying in a cave to a dead fish on a cross.

As I said, losing the life of the community, the lonely individual acquired the fear of uncertainty. In order to aleviate this fear, the human mind invented, and continues to invent, all kinds of divinations, astrology, fortune telling and superstitious rituals.

The new era also brought alcoholism, drugs, intoxication, corruption, perversities, rape, sadism, torture, resentfulness, envy, jealousy, vindictiveness, fanaticism, obsessions, obstinacy, intolerance, ideological or religious persecutions and wars. It brought that dangerous abnormality, hatred.

The new era brought nastiness, malevolence and malignity.

Most adolescent-minded people are discontented with themselves. They are discontented with themselves whenever they become aware of the gap between their pretentious ego and their real self, whenever they think they deserve more than they achieve. Most of these try to discharge the psychosomatic arousals created by their discontentment with themselves into discontent and anger with others, into nastiness, or malignity. There is no nastiness, or malignity in the animal world, simply because animals never develop pretentiousness.

When we are nasty to others, in reality we are trying to punish our true self for failing its ideal ego. Occasionally one has the impression that those who persevere in being nasty to others are, in fact, trying to provoke their own punishment, the punishment of their pretentiousness and caprices. Deep down, perhaps, they feel that only by punishing their pretentiousness and caprices can they reach contentment or happiness.

The new style of life also brought cardiovascular problems, psychosomatic diseases and mental disorders. Later it will be explained that these problems, diseases and disorders mainly belong to the adolescent mentality.

Having inhibited or eliminated natural maturity, the adolescent mentality created its own. The supreme aim of the adolescent was to appear grown up. An abstract 'ought to be' became the guideline to adulthood.

The immaturity of adolescent-minded humanity can be best seen in their unpredictability and in their inconsistency. We are able to jump from love to hatred, from charity to genocide.

Following the 'ought to be' maturity, adolescents started assuming roles, affectations, poses, appearances, simulations, pomposity or solemnity. An individual became a 'persona', meaning a mask in Latin. Life gave the impression of being 'le bal masqué', as Stendhal pointed out. Poses, affectations and masquerades developed a stage fright which increased the arrogance and aggression of the adolescent mentality. Men invented ideas such as decorum, mannerism and fashion, and started being ruled by them. We now live in an over-decorated world.

With its over-seriousness, its pretentiousness, its poses and affectations, its unnatural and artificial world created by an immature way of thinking, full of absurdities, incongruities, and paradoxes, the adolescent mentality brought another novelty in nature: ridicule. We are proud, and often emphasise the fact that we are the only species capable of laughter, but few have pointed out that we are also the only laughable species. We are laughable whenever we are guided by supernatural ideas, beliefs, prejudices, pretentiousness or affectations. When asked his reason for laughter, Democritus answered: 'I laugh at vanity and infatuation which rule people... I laugh at men's being devoured by ambition, taking great trouble for a little of glory or admiration'.

Other animals, children, naturally mature men and women are only laughable when they imitate the adolescent mentality or behave in accordance with its style of life.

Those ruled by the adolescent mentality must know that they are laughable because they spend so much energy on trying to impress, to seduce or to bewilder. What is even more comic is that, with all manner of art and artistry, man tries to impress women, as he fears their derision of his mind's invented roles more than anything else. A woman who is ruled by the adolescent mentality can be even more ridiculous than man; she usually tries to impress herself, as she fears the derision of her own mind by her innate common-sense intelligence.

This adolescent mentality established itself so strongly that by now we consider it the one and only human mentality, that it is innate, and that it belongs to the human species as a whole, to men and women, to old and young, and to the mature and the immature. By now many are convinced that the present way of thinking and believing always was and always will be, the same.

The society organised by the adolescent mentality became a powerful incentive to the development of the mind, therefore to the successful establishment of the adolescent style of thinking and living throughout the world. The mind noticeably evolved in the last two and a half thousand years because the society organised by the adolescent mentality was, and still is, a society in which rootless individuals were ruthlessly competing in exploiting or out-manoeuvering each other. The new mentality's wickedness became a major incentive to the development of the mind's craftiness. This remarkable progress of the human mind took place, however, at the expense of the brain's other activity: intelligence. What is more, the cleverer the mind became, the more frightened of others' cleverness it became.

Natural selection started being influenced by cleverness, craftiness and aggressiveness, all inspired by the mind.

That my theory about adolescent revolutions may have a certain validity can also be deduced from the fact that ideas such as guilt and original sin are deeply rooted in the human mind. What else could have inspired these ideas but the adolescent revolution's destruction of the natural order and fears brought on by a life based on artificially created rules and laws.

In fact, it is in the nature of usurpation to produce remorse and nostalgia. Ever since the adolescent revolution, nostalgia has become part of human existence. Going back through history it is obvious that each generation looked back romantically or tenderly on a past era. One has the impression that we face life walking backwards, the eyes of our mind turned towards the good old days.

Some social or religious rituals aim to solve the problem of nostalgia by trying to urge people back into the life of a happy community by the administration of Holy Communion, or by passing around a marijuana cigarette. This can only provoke amusement and laughter.

AMUSEMENT AND LAUGHTER

What is laughter?

This is a question which has probably intrigued man ever since he started asking questions.

'The greatest of thinkers, from Aristotle downward, have tackled this little problem which has a knack of baffling every effort, of slipping away and escaping only to bob up again; a pert challenge flung at philosophic speculation.' This quote from Bergson hints at the difficulties.

The following theories quoted by H.J.Eysenck in his introduction to 'The Psychology of Humour', edited by J.H.Golstein and P.E.Mcghee, further illustrate our confusion about laughter.

'Biological, Instinct and Evolutional Theories' explain that laughter is a 'built-in' system which has a utilitarian purpose.

'Superiority Theories' indicate that laughter is a personal triumph. Thomas Hobbes (1588-1679), a well-known supporter of this theory, in his 'Human Nature' wrote: 'And in this case the passion of laughter preceedeth from sudden imagination of our oddes and eminency; for what is else the recommending of ourselves to our own good opinion, by comparison with another man's infirmity or absurdity?' Hobbes also said: 'Sudden glory is the passion which maketh those grimaces called Laughter'.

'Incongruity Theories' insist that laughter is caused by unusual, inconsistent or incompatible pairing of ideas, situations, behaviour or attitudes.

'Surprise Theories' claim that the essential element of laughter is suddenness and the unexpected.

'Ambivalence Theories' say that laughter is a reaction to the simultaneousness of two incompatible or contradictory emotions.

'Configurational Theories' explain laughter as the perception of a certain connection among elements which appear unrelated or incongruous.

'Release and Relief Theories' state that laughter is caused by relief from tension.

'The Psychoanalytical Theory' stresses that 'pleasure derived from ' ... 'proceeds from a saving in expenditure of affect', as Freud wrote. 'Obviously what is fine about it', he continued, 'is the triumph of narcissism, the ego's victorious assertion of its own vulnerability. It refuses to be hurt by the arrows of reality or to be compelled to suffer '...' It signifies the triumph, not only of the ego, but also of the pleasure principle, which is strong enough to assert itself here in face of adverse circumstances.'

In my view, amusement and laughter are intimately connected with the world of apprehension and fears created by the mind and its over-seriousness. Over-seriousness is not the opposite of ridicule, it is ridicule, it is the very source of amusement and laughter.

The ridiculous began when we abandoned nature in favour of supernature, when we settled in cloud-cuckoo land and started leaning on illusions, when we escaped from reality into the mind's world of beliefs, wishfulness, absurd hopes or undeserved expectations.

'What excellent fools religion makes of men', wrote Ben Jonson. He could have added that it is not only religion, but any other of the mind's creations, when taken over-seriously, that makes fools of us.

Any perception of the discrepancy between affectations and reality, between the mind's 'ought to be' and nature's 'to be', between ambition and achievement, promise and fulfillment, between the mind's logic and common-sense logic, can create amusement and laughter. Any violation, distortion or debasement of the sacred taboos, any collapse of superstitions, prejudices or beliefs, any degradation of our affectations, roles or pomposity can cause amusement and laughter.

In fact, we are amused and we laugh whenever the over-seriousness of the mind's inventions is shaken or degraded.

Why should this be?

Eliminating this over-seriousness, and therefore liberating ourselves of the fears that the mind's over-seriousness create, we eliminate the source of psychosomatic emotional arousal. Cutting off the source of this arousal, the existing arousal which was accumulated in our body, is discharged, usually taking the form of laughter. Without the emotional arousal, which implies tension and stress, we experience a biological well-being, which we translate in terms of pleasure and amusement.

In physiological terms, amusement and laughter are a result of a healthier balance between activities of the sympathetic and parasympathetic systems, and the reduction in activity of the adrenal glands, produced by the elimination of the mind's fears.

In the new balance between the sypathetic and parasympathetic systems the activity of the former is reduced and that of the latter increased, and this improves our state of existence. Amusement and laughter, in fact, can be accompanied by the brightenning or sparkling of the eyes, by weeping, increased salivation and even uncontrolled urinating. These are all activities under the control of the parasympathetic nervous system.

At the same time, due to the diminished activity of the sympathetic nervous system, contraction of the smooth muscles diminishes, reducing stress and tension.

A more balanced activity of the adrenal glands, created by the elimination of the mind's fears, distends the voluntary muscles and normalises the blood preasure.

With a diminished activity of the sympathetic system and adrenal glands, the blood vessels of the brain, retina, and kidneys become less contracted, allowing these organs to work better.

The reduced activity of the sympathetic nervous system can bring our body's rigidity to such flexibility as to force us to collapse when siezed by uncontrollable laughter.

By analysing an affectation, this popular creation of our mind, I hope to illustrate my theory better.

An affectation creates a state of precariousness and fear which produces a certain emotional arousal. This arousal makes for potential aggression. Anybody's affectation, therefore, frightens us, mainly producing apprehension or uneasiness. Intuitively we feel that people hanging on their mind's inventions are in danger, and we sense that people in danger can be dangerous. This fear caused by the affectations of others, provokes a certain emotional arousal in us, increasing our tension and stress.

When the affectations of others are debased or shaken, we rid ourselves of the fear of them. By eliminating this fear, we cut off the source of the emotional arousal. By cutting of the source of the emotional arousal, we become able to discharge the existing accumulated emotional arousal, mainly in the form of laughter, thereby reaching a pleasant biological feeling.

A healthier balance between the activities of the sympathetic and parasympathetic systems, and a more normal activity of the adrenal glands, brings us from tension to relaxation, from rigidity to flexibility. A feeling of warmth and well-being invades our bodies. No-one described this better than Baudelaire, when he explained that laughter is 'la joie de grandir.'

Every aspect of our mind's world of beliefs and fantasies is potentially ridiculous. The ridiculous, like beauty, however, is in the eye of the beholder.

Two artificially created institutions of the adolescent mentality, that of the husband and that of the political or religious authority, have always been a major source of the ridiculous. As Chamfort said: 'Without the government, France would not laugh any more.'

The perception of the ridiculous can be helped by jokes, anecdotes, caricatures, parodies, comedies, and so on...

Jokes make us laugh when they shake the mind's threatening over-seriousness. Obscene jokes usually try to degrade inhibiting moral values concerning sex. Practical jokes provoke laughter when they succeed in shaking people's intimidating poses of solemnity or dignity.

Caricatures and parodies induce laughter when they debase a feared authority or power. A caricature or a parody of a dead or over-thrown dictator seldom makes us laugh. Even the debasing of external signs of authority or power, or the humiliation of social status symbols, such as a bird defecating on a Rolls-Royce, can create amusement or laughter.

Chaos, or the 'infinite agility of chaos', to use an expression of Schlegel, can provoke laughter, as it derides a tiring socially or morally imposed discipline.

Frivolity, flippancy or coquetry induce amusement and laughter when they shake the menacing rigidity of our affected behaviour or attitudes. A foreigner's affectations or poses can also expose the ridiculous in our own affectations and poses.

Imitations of boasters makes us laugh as it debases their bragging.

By bringing proud, distinguished and successful men or women to more human levels, anecdotes can be refreshing.

When an alarming or strain provoking hypocrisy is exposed, it can create mirth.

The derision of pretentious snobbery is also satisfying.

When breaking oppressive formality or conventions, clumsiness or awkwardness can be enjoyable.

Attenuating our fear of God, stories of the devil are often a relief.

Playing on the rigidity of language, spoonerisms and puns produce laughter.

Shaking the tension created by over-seriousness, slapstick can be hilarious. Deflating blustering infatuation, humbling dangerous arrogance, defaming the portentousness of the famous, defeating the terror of aggression, demoting an abusive class consciousness, profaning the intimidating sacred, de-mystifying the dreaded occult, can all create amusement and laughter.

By challenging the mind's established order without malice or malevolence, a comedian can give pleasure and contentment. A comedian and a revolutionary have one thing in common: they both challenge the established order. The difference is, however, that while the former tries to shake it, the latter tries to replace it with a new order, another frame of mind, another ridiculous world. A dedicated comedian is never revolutionary, while a dedicated revolutionary is always comic.

The fact that the readiness to laugh increases with the increase in togetherness and group density, proves that amusement and laughter are a result of victory over fear. Isolated and lonely individuals lose a certain quantity and intensity of their fears when in a group, above all when there is a feeling of group belonging.

One kind of laughter, however, needs particular attention: the laughter of infants.

In my theory that laughter is a form of the discharge of our emotional arousals caused by fears, is right, then we could ask ourselves how could children of a tender and innocent age acquire emotional arousals and tensions?

The answer to this question is that we inherit fears. Like other animals during gestation, we inherit the fears of our species, and also the fears that particularly worried our mother during her pregnancy.

As I said, emotional arousals, tension and stress are results of an extra quantity of the neuro-transmitters of the sympathetic nervous system and of the adrenal hormones in our blood stream. During embriogenesis, these neuro-transmitters and hormones created by a strong and persistent psychosomatic arousal in the mother, can pass into the embryo, influencing its development, and predisposing the progeny to the fear or fears which impressed the mother.

In play a child liberates himself from inherited fears. Liberating himself from these fears, a child develops exuberance and laughter. If tossed in the air and safely caught, a child will laugh as he has succeeded in playing with his inherited fear of falling. Playing on inarticulated screams, eliminates the child's inherited fear of screams. Screams frighten many species as they represent a sign of the risen or rising emotional arousal, therefore a sign of a potential aggression or a charge. A child laughs when successful in playing on excess or exaggeration, as this placates his inherited fear of them.

Perhaps boys' passion for playing with toys representing war-weapons is their search to alieviate their fear of war which they inherited from their mothers who procreated in an atmosphere of war, ever since the adolescent revolution.

A type of laughter which has always intrigued is the laughter that accompanies bad news, often even news of the death of someone we love.

This mainly occurs when the particular news has been

anticipated or dreaded for some time. Fearing or expecting bad news creates an emotional arousal, strain or tension. When the bad news finally arrives, the suffering of the mind which was perpetuated by the dread, disappears, creating liberation of the existing arousals through laughter.

When we escape from danger, especially mortal danger, and when we suddenly realise how lucky we are, our assumed roles, affectations and poses vanish for a while, giving way to a 'fou rire'.

Laughter is often used artificially, conventionally or hypocritically. Like any other artificial creation of our mind, this calculated laughter becomes a laughting matter when its purpose fails.

There are some illnesses, such as epilepsy and tetanus which cause spontaneous laughter. They have the reduction of over-seriousness in common. The over-serious adolescent mentality can also be shaken by the use of alcohol or marijuana, or even strychnine poisoning, creating conditions for laughter.

One type of laughter, laughter caused by tickling, has been puzzling students of this problem for years.

I think that we lough when tickled because someone is playing with our innate defensiveness by gently touching the parts of our body supplied with protective reflexes. When someone plays with these parts of our body, our inherited fears are reduced or eliminated, allowing the existing emotional arousal, created by these fears, to be discharged in the form of laughter.

Tickling can produce annoyance, suffering, violent withdrawal of the tickled parts, indifference, pleasure, and laughter. The reaction of the tickled person depends on three factors: The first is the state of playfulness of the tickled. The second is the state of playfulness of the tickler. The third is the state of emotional predisposition of the tickled towards the tickler. If the tickled person is in a state of playfulness, the tickling will produce pleasure and laughter as long as the other two factors are positive. If the tickler is not in a state of playfulness, he will be unable to play properly with the parts of the body supplied with protective reflexes, which will produce a negative reaction from the tickled person. If the tickled person either dislikes or distrusts the tickler, even the most delicate caress will produce neither laughter nor pleasure.

HUMOUR

'In truth, there is nothing so unsettled and uncertain as our notion of humour in general', Fielding wrote in his 'Covent Garden Journal No.19.'

Our understanding of this subject has not improved since Fielding's times. The fact that many people consider humour as a kind of synonym to the comic and wit, has merely added to the confusion.

Perhaps, it would be easier to explain the nature of humour if we were first to define the comic.

In my view, the comic is whatever helps us to liberate ourselves from mind created fears and worries. Whenever physical laws or cosmic order degrade our mind's abstractions or beliefs, whenever nature deflates super-nature, whenever reality debases our pretentiousness, capricious expectations, or wishful assumptions, whenever material objectivity brings ethereal subjectivity and its poses, affectations or self-deceptions, to the ground, briefly, whenever our mind's world is shaken, the comic comes into existence.

What does humour really mean, then?

The word humour comes from the Latin word 'umor' and the medevial word 'humor', both of which were medical terms meaning a biological disposition or temperament.

From the beginning of the Seventeenth-Century, however, the word humour also began to mean an adopted 'umor', an affectation, a pose, which became a source of the laughable. In the Introduction of his 'Every Man out of his Humour', Ben Jonson found the affected 'umor' 'more than most ridiculous'. This confused humour with the comic.

In order to give a more accurate description of humour, we should go back to its original meaning.

In my opinion, humour is basically a realistic vision or perception of the world around us. This realistic vision or perception is the result of what we call a sense of humour. A sense of humour is a state of our brain's activity under certain hormonal and neuro-humoural body's conditions. A sense of humour's vision, perception and reasoning are, in fact, results of our brain's activity in the optimal range of our emotional arousals, of our brain's activity in the absence of emotional arousals created by the mind's fears, frustrations, worries, discontents and sufferings, in the absence of a threatened and vulnerable idealized ego.

Without the mind's self-created fears, frustrations, worries, discontents and sufferings, without an idealized ego, we find the world created by the mind's wishful speculations or fantasies, built around a self-inflated ego, as humorous.

The only way to see the world around us realistically, would be to eliminate our 'ought to be' ego, to organise our aspirations around our real self. We must never forget that most of our discontent and unhappiness is mainly caused by the gap between the capricious pretentions of our self-inflated ego and the abilties of our real self to materialize these pretentions.

We can acquire a sense of humour by playing with our ego and its pretentions, by taking our affectations, poses or assumed personalities, as a joke, by not considering our over-seriousness seriously, by developing a sense of self-ridicule. People who do not exaggerate their self-importance, who realise that cemetaries are filled with those who considered themselves indispensable, are those with a sense of humour. 'A sense of humour keen enough to show a man his own absurdities as well as those of other people's', stressed Samuel Butler in his 'Life and Habit'.

With self-ridicule, we also eliminate that terrible fear, the fear of making fools of ourselves, of appearing ridiculous. 'No-one is laughable who laughs at himself,' Seneca suggested. Persecuted by the fear of making a fool of oneself, one becomes ridiculous as one reacts over-seriously.

By liberating our perceiving system from the deformation and inhibition created by over-seriousness, a sense of humour enables us to perceive humanity in its nakedness, therefore with magnaminity. Carlyle understood this when, in his 'On Richter', he wrote: 'The essence of humour is sensibility: warm, tender fellow-feeling with all forms of existence.'

With a sense of humour, we cannot be but magnanimous as it helps us to realize that a great deal of ridicule consists of human suffering, a pathetic despair, brought about through pretentiousness, through the chase of 'ought to be' illusion, created by capricious over-ambition.

A sense of humour not only liberates our rational and realistic reasoning from the intimidation of irrational wishful thinking, but it also keeps the intelligent activity of our brain alert and alive.

A sense of humour also establishes a more harmonious relationship between the old brain and the new, which is made more and more difficult by the precarious and threatened imaginary world of the mind.

Being infectous, a sense of humour can create a healthy atmosphere of intimacy and togetherness, so important for our species, born to live in a community.

Immunizing us against ideologies or beliefs, dogmas or prejudices, a sense of humour enables us to live in real freedom, freedom from stress and frustrations.

A sense of humour, therefore, is the only way we can emerge from a life dominated by the mind's fears and sufferings. Only with a sense of humour can we free ourselves from the depressing adolescent mentality, and achieve that of natural maturity.

There is more of a sense of humour among the English than among other nationalities. I think that this is mainly due to the following three factors.

Firstly, by cultural tradition and intuition, the English tend to prefer pragmatism, possibilism and practicality than ideologies, wishful fantasies and rigid beliefs. There is reduced possibility of developing an idealized or self-opininated ego in pragmatism. Without an idealized ego, there is less of the mind's created fears, therefore less of the psychosomatic emotional arousals. A reduced amount of these emotional arousals has allowed the English to develop their experimental reasoning, their common sense and their sense of humour.

Secondly, the English brought their village mentality into the towns, and kept this mentality alive with clubs. The village mentality tends to deride self-infatuation or conceit.

The third factor which allowed England to enjoy a sense of humour for centuries was that they got rid of their humourless, arrogant and conceited element. This pretentious group were only too happy to settle in the colonies where they would feel important.

Owing to its brilliance, wit is often mistaken for humour. I would like to explain my view of the difference between the two.

Wit is a product of our brain's activity in conditions of a certain mind's created emotional arousal, originated and usually kept alive by resentment, resentment generally caused by a wit's offended or humiliated ego.

In the discharge of his emotional arousal, a wit is usually vindictive or malicious. 'There is no possibility of being witty without a little of ill-nature; the malice of a good thing is the barb that makes it stick,' wrote Sheridan in 'School for Scandal'.

In launching his poisonous arrows, a wit never misses an oportunity. Quintilian expressed this inclination when he said: 'Potius amicum quam dictum perdere,' meaning that a wit prefers to lose a friend than a witty remark.

When a wit's emotional arousal is placed at the service of the idea that created it, then wit becomes a compulsory game. 'Plagued with an itching leprosy of wit,' wrote Ben Jonson in 'Every Man out of his Humour'.

In his bitterness, intoxicated by the venom of his emotional arousal, more often than not, a wit likes to poison the lives of his victims. He revels in tormenting his targets. Swift, a well-known representative of malicious wit, confessed to Pope that it was a pleasure to harrass people. 'The chief end I propose to myself in all my labours is to vex the world rather than to divert it.' In his 'Antologie de l'humour noir', André Breton, describing Alphonse Allais, perhaps the greates malicious wit in France since Voltaire, explains: 'Il (Allais) excelle à mettre en dificulté l'individu satisfait, ébloui de truisme et sûr de lui'...

While humour creates relaxation, wit creates tension; while humour produces togetherness and playfulness, wit produces division and distance; while humour generates charm, benevolence and magnanimity, wit generates defiance, malevolence and contempt; while humour disarms the mind, wit alerts it; while humour seeks intimacy, wit longs for indiscretion; while humour brings about humility, wit brings about insolence; while humour gives rise to tolerance, wit gives rise to impatience and impertinence; while humour leads to kindness, wit often offends. As Pope stressed in his 'Essay of Criticism': 'Great wits sometimes may gloriously offend.'

Charles Brooks, in his 'On the Difference between Wit and Humour' (in the book 'I was Just Thinking', edited by E.Parker), wrote: 'Humorous persons have pleasant mouths turned up at the corners...But the mouth of a merely witty man is hard and sour until the moment of its discharge.'

THE MATURE WAY OF REASONING

'The power set free from the atom has changed everything, except our way of thinking,' stressed Einstein.

We tend to resign ourselves to the fact that our present way of thinking is the only one that we are capable of. Many people agree with Claude Levi-Strauss that all humanity, throughout time and space, have a bipolar, oppositional structure of thinking in common.

In my view, this dualistic and antagonistic way of thinking is not characteristic of humanity in general, but of those who are ruled by the adolescent mentality. The either/or way of thinking is that of the mind's created fears. Any extreme 'either' is our mind's escape from a frightening 'or'. In this escape, however, our fear of the opposite extreme increases. This increased fear builds up a psychosomatic arousal which we usually try to discharge by destroying or fighting the extreme opposite. Many religions and ideologies, these hopeful shelters from the 'cruel' reality, adopted Christ's motto: 'Whosoever is not with me is against me.'

The sad thing is that people ruled by the either/or way of thinking can never find peace of mind even if they succeed in eliminating those who in their opinion represent the opposite. By eliminating its enemies, the mind becomes haunted by their ghosts. In the kingdom of the mind, ghosts are privileged citizens.

The either/or way of thinking found its best representatives in philosophers such as Aristotle, Hegel and Marx. The Hegelian-Marxist theory of contradictions dominates present-day philosophysing.

Marx insisted that reality was a confrontation of extremes, that every thesis was opposed by an antithesis.

If Marx had analysed the origin of the energy which gave life to theses and antitheses, and what made them so arrogant and aggressive, he would have realised that they only exist in our mind. Both theses and antitheses are hypotheses. Creating a precarious state of existence, hypotheses produce a psychosomatic emotional arousal. This arousal provides the driving force to both theses and antitheses. Dialectic tension, therefore, is created by the mind and its fears, by an immature mentality.

The Marxist theory insists that progress is a result of dialectic tension or attrition between two opposing extremes. In fact, Marx is right, but only as far as the progress of the human mind is concerned. Operating in the world organised by abstract speculations, the human mind was forced into a permanent juggling act, a continuous fantastic pyrotecnic al exercise.

As I stressed before, this progress of the human mind's abilities has been at the expense of our brain's intelligent activity, our mature reasoning, and our mental and physical health.

By deriding both extremes, a sense of humour helps us to discover that between the dogmatic either/or, there is a vast continuum of intermediate existences, a multi-reality world. By not taking seriously the over-seriousness of the dialectical way of thinking, we would find that between the two mutually intolerant and aggressive extreme probabilities there is a chain of peaceful and co-existing certainties. As Coleridge said: In humour the little is made great and the great little, in order to destroy both.'

The best way to shake the two extremes would be to introduce a third dimension between the dialectic contradictions.

It is interesting to note that thoughout history, the human mind has only inserted a third dimension into the either/or way of thinking, once. In the XIII Century, the Catholic Church introduced Purgatory between Heaven and Hell. In their over-seriousness, however, the Protestants ignored it.

The neither/nor of the either/or way of thinking could become an important instrument of third dimension reasoning. Guided by the neither/nor, we would see neither one side of a coin nor the other, but the coin as a whole.

Every generation produces certain wise people who introduce a flexible third dimension into their reasoning. They are usually, however, classified as eccentrics, disbelievers, heretics, deviationists, dissidents, comedians or humourists, and are often persecuted or eliminated.

A sense of humour reasoning could replace our present presumptuous knowing and judging with a more realistic understanding and tolerance.

With a sense of humour reasoning, an objective truth, which in our present way of thinking has no aggression behind it, might acquire considerable power, the power of deriding dialectic extremes.

A sense of humour could teach us to learn from experience, from our errors and failures.

In their self-rightousness, people with an adolescent mentality are seldom wrong. For any of their faults or errors of judgement, there is always a scapegoat. Self-blame does not occur to an adolescent. A believer prefers to see reality wrong than to admit to a deficiency of his beliefs.

In order to take the present way of thinking more humourously, we could remind ourselves of those few lines by William James. In his opinion, dialectic thinking can be seen as a creation of the 'pantomime-state of mind'. In the pantomime all common things are represented to happen in impossible ways, people jump down each other's throats, houses are turned inside out, old women become young men, "everything passes into its opposite" with inconceivable celerity and skill..,' he wrote.

In order to take our present way of thinking even more humourously, I would like to point out the following: The purpose of reasoning in nature is to solve alarming situations or emergencies more efficiently. Our present way of thinking, however, has created a permanent state of alarming emergency, a constant escape.

Our current way of thinking and of behaving produces our world of irony.

Like most people, Kierkegaard thought that irony was a permanent part of our life.

The 'irony of fate' belongs to the world of faith, the world of credulities, illusions and wishful expectations. We are not victims of irony, we are makers of irony. We are makers of irony whenever we consider ourselves above the laws of nature, above true fate.

Inspired by wishful fantasies, our expectations are permanently exposed to the danger of being mocked.

The continuous presence of irony in human life is the best evidence that there may be some truth in my theory that something must be wrong with our present way of thinking and perceiving.

The only way of solving the problem of irony is with a sense of humour. By increasing our perception, a sense of humour will decrease our deception.

A sense of humour could also help us to become good sports. By eliminating the fear of losing, we acquire power over irony. In Medieval Italy there was the following popular saying: 'The three most powerful people in the world are: the Pope, the Emperor and the good loser.'

EMOTIONS, MEMORY AND A SENSE OF HUMOUR

We glorify ourselves for going to the moon, but we know very little in fields which could improve life on earth, such as that of memory.

No-one knows what kind of biological or electric activities take place in our brain when we memorize and then evoke the past. Most people explain that the memory implies the capacity to register events brought by the sensory system to our brain, and to revive them in our consciousness on subsequent occasions.

Perhaps, we could understand, and, therefore, use our memory better if we analysed the energy which operates it. Forming or reviving memories are activities, and activities imply energy.

To become a part of our memory, information or happenings have to pass through the phases of stimulation, sensation and perception.

For a stimulation to become a sensation, it has to be absorbed by our senses. To be stimulated by events, one has to be in a state of excitability. A stimulation cannot reach the phase of sensation if our senses are not sensitive, if they are not in a state of alertness, apprehension or vigilance.

'Receptor activation requires that a stimulus be of suitable intensity as well as of suitable quality,' we read in text-books dealing with the nervous system and memory. In order to be activated by a stimulus, a receptor certainly needs to be in a state of receptiveness, in a state of suitable alertness. What is more, the intensity of a stimulus depends on the intensity of the alertness of our

53

sense-perception system. The same stimulus can be sensed and perceived by the same person in different ways on different occasions.

A sensation only becomes a perception after having been scrutinized and valued by our brain. In order to be able to perceive a sensation, our brain must be in a state of perceptiveness.

States of aliveness and vivacity of our senses and states of perceptiveness of our brain are dynamic states, states of activity, states of energy.

Each living being is in a fluctuating state of existence, and each state of existence has its own level of awareness and perceptiveness.

What is it that provides the energy needed for the alertness of our senses and the perceptiveness of our brain, for openness to new events, and readiness for new experiences?

In my view, this energy is provided by the basic fears we inherit as a species, and as an individual of that species. As I stressed before, fears are the principal source of bio-energy.

In fact, when we need to increase this bio-energy in people and animals, we try to frighten them. Shouting orders in threatening tones, sergeants and officers aim to increase the nervous energy of their soldiers, thus enabling them to execute the orders. We beat or whip animals to improve their performance. By some curious sylogism or analogy, we even kick cars or television sets, when they are faulty, hoping to make them work!

The energy produced by feelings of vulnerability and fears, enables our senses to detect the stimulus, and our brain to perceive the sensation.

Fluctuating in their intensity with the changes in our internal milieu and the external environment, our feelings of vulnerability and our fears provide us with a constant change in our states of energy. Variations in the degrees of our alertness and perceptiveness are directly related to the variations in the degree of our feelings of vulnerability and in our fears.

As in the rest of the animal world, our basic feelings of vulnerability and fears are mainly caused by physiological discomforts and needs. We differ from other animals, however, because a great variety of our feelings of vulnerability and fears are self-inflicted, the main ones being those created by our escape from reality into the precarious world of the mind. We are able to develop that brooding fear of toppling from an idealized world of our mind into an unflattering reality.

The energy created by feelings of vulnerability and fears helps us to develop and to keep our curiosity and interest alive.

What provides the energy which enables a perceived information to be registered in our brain, to become a part of our memory?

Emotional arousals provide the necessary energy for the memorization of events. Any information perceived by the brain will be registered in our memory pool on the wave-length of the emotional arousal it creates, on the frequency of energy this information produces in contact with the existing emotional arousal created by the extent of fears at the moment immediately preceding the information. In essence, our memories are a network of pathways of energy left on the brain by different levels of emotional arousals.

Both rewarding or punishing events, and exciting or inhibiting conditioning, used to facilitate memorization and learning, in fact, create emotional arousals without which there would be no memorization or learning.

That the memory is associated with emotions can be deduced from the fact that when the emotional centres of our brain (the limbic system and hypothalamus) are damaged, or inhibited, the registration of new events, or the recollection of past experiences, are considerably reduced.

The same brain cells register many memories, all recorded on the different intensities of emotional energy.

The brain cells dealing with the memory must be intimately connected with those dealing with vision, because most information is stored in the brain in the form of images, pictures or figures.

Given the interconnection of all the cells of the brain, the messages provided to it not only by our sight, but also by other senses, often take the form of images. Blind people's memory is made up mostly of kinaesthetic-tactile images.

The intimate connection of the cells dealing with the memory with those dealing with vision must have enabled us to create mental visualization, analogies and metaphores, essential for our imaginative way of thinking. Aristotle was right when he said: 'The act of understanding is always accompanied by imaginative activity.'

By stimulating vision centres, our wishful ideas and fantasies also take the shapes of images. It is by creating emotional arousals that our imagination can stimulate the vision centres in our brain and become a part of our memory. Even the most absurd speculations representing things which do not exist in reality are visualized by our inner eye. We all have, for example, a certain picture of hell and paradise. Dante depicted them both colourfully and graphically. Many people have vivid visions of their Utopias. By persistently stimulating our vision centre, a strong emotional arousal can even provoke mystic apparitions or the appearances of ghosts.

Before becoming part of our memory, any new information is analysed and assessed by our brain either with the logic of our intellect, or with the interest of our mind, in the light of past experiences registered on the same level of the emotional arousal that the new information creates. If the new information has been analysed and assessed with the logic of our intellect, and in the light of past experiences classified by our intellect, the new information will be registered as a concept, a concept reflecting an objective reality. If, instead, the new information has been analysed and assessed by our brain with the dominant interest of the mind, and in the light of past experiences classified by our mind's wishfulness, the new information will be registered in our memory as an opinion or a belief, an assumption or an hypothesis.

How are past experiences evoked from our memory?

Events registered in our brain are best revived by the flow of our emotional arousals similar in their intensity to those which originally encrusted the events. The recall of past experiences from our memory pool is a kind of echo in the form of mental images, of photograms, provoked by a wave of energy of an emotional arousal.

That the revival of past experiences is provoked by emotional arousals is best illustrated by dreams. Most dreams take place during REM (Rapid Eye Movements) periods of sleep when arousal threshold is significantly increased, when the sympathetic nervous system, this main source of emotional arousals, is noticeably active. During REM dreams we can observe the reaction of people's eyes, faces or bodies to their emotional arousals. We are not frightened by what we see in nightmares, we have them because we are in a state of fear.

It has been claimed that even infants in utero, without any past experience, have REM sleeps and dreams. In my opinion, this can only be explained by emotional arousals passed to them by their mothers.

One's memory can even be revived by external energy. Electrical stiumlation of parts of the brain can revive events which were registered by a similar wavelength of emotional energy.

It is well known that people suffer severe pain in a leg or arm that has been amputated, or cramps in the stomach when the ulcer has long been cured. This usually happens when people experience the same level of emotional arousal on which these pains were registered in their memory.

Students who did their homework with blaring background music have difficulty remembering what they have learned in the cold silence of a school hall. We revive our learned material better if we acquire the same emotional arousals in which the learning originally took place.

When sober, people have difficulty remembering events which occurred when they were drunk or drugged. Their memory may return, however, when they reach the same state of intoxication, carrying the same emotional arousals.

Deep-sea divers sometimes have difficulty recalling underwater experiences when back on the surface.

Many insist that a 'retrieval clue' can help the access to the memory. This is true, but only when this 'retrieval clue' creates the level of emotional arousal on which it was previously registered in our memory.

If one learns a foreign language in a concentration camp, for example, one may have difficulty using it at a social or flippant conversation during a dinner party. If the subject of conversation is the war, stress or deprivations, however, the language will be much more fluent.

Re-instating the circumstances in which certain events took place helps recall the events. Proust's emotional arousal caused by 'the taste of the crumb of madeleine soaked in her concoction of lime flowers', which revived memories of his childhood, illustrates this.

We do not lose our memory with old age so much because of the reduced efficiency of our brain. We mostly lose it because in ageing, we lose the ability or desire to experience certain emotions, which inhibits the recollection of the memories registered with these emotions.

Alcoholics have difficulty acquiring both new memories, and reviving old ones, because the activity of the emotional centres in their brains are noticeably reduced.

Tranquillizers can inhibit the efficiency of our memory because they reduce our emotional arousals below their beneficial effects.

The mind is able to create high emotional arousals when it wants to forget unpleasant or offending experiences. Some people with inflated egos can develop hatred for their benefactors. With the increased emotional arousal, created by this hatred, they can forget their benefactors or their benefactors' deeds.

During a particularly strong emotional crisis certain people are able to escape into partial or total amnesia, sometimes reaching a stage in which they do not even remember who they are.

In terror our perceptive system can become paralysed. We seldom remember events immediately preceding terrifying accidents.

The life of an individual is a chain of temporary states of energy. This fluctuation is mainly governed by the activity of the sympathetic system. The sympathetic and parasympathetic systems usually operate simultaneously, balancing their activities in accordance with the circumstances of the given moment. Changing easily, these balancing activities provide us with a wide range of emotional arousals, a wide variety of emotional states. We are constantly jumping from one unsteady state of energy to another, from one fluctuating emotional state to another, from one set of memories to another.

What we call an association of events in our brain is usually caused by a succession of emotional states. Newly perceived information revives events which were registered previously in our memory on the wavelength of emotional energy that the newly perceived information creates. One of these revived events can trigger off another emotional arousal with which it has been associated on a different occasion, evoking from our memory-storage events and persons, animals or landscapes, registered with that intensity of the emotional arousal of that particular occasion, and so on, thus creating a succession of images and ideas in our head.

In dreams, this succession of events, caused by a chain of emotional arousals in REM sleep, are often in their purest state. During fully awakened consciousness the interest of the mind, or the logic of our intellect, tends to put them in order, into a coherent succession of visual imageries.

In essence, we are permanently, even if often only marginally, another being, a different personality. Each state of existence relates to the external world in accordance with its fears and its discomforts of each specific moment. Each state of existence has its own balance between the sympathetic and parasympathetic systems, its own hormonal activity, its own memory, its own brain's state, its own mental activity, its own logic and reasoning. A state of existence can easily be influenced even by a slight change in the body's temperature. Many feverish tubercular people's mental states create lyrical or poetic ways of thinking. High fever can create hallucinations.

Each state of existence of a person only perceives that which is in his/her best interest at that moment, but which may not coincide with the best interest of his/her next state of existence. We often suddenly notice something useful, surprised that we had never noticed it before, although it had always been around us.

Each state of existence revives events from past experiences which are registered on that existence's level of emotional arousal. For instance, we see our parents in a variety of ways depending on the state of existence in which we remember them. In occasions of failure we may see them in a negative light, because failures evoke unpleasant experiences from the past. In moments of success and glory, however, we might remember them in a positive light, as happiness revives pathways engraved on our brain with pleasant experiences. Our past life is like a library where we select books or magazines which appeal to us at that particular moment.

The emotional states of other animals are mainly created by biological discomforts or needs, by fluctuation in their bodies' natural rhythms and hormonal activity, or by information obtained from the external world by their sensory and perceiving systems.

Humans experience many more emotional states than other species. We are seldom consciously aware of most of them, and even less of their subtle differences. A great variety of these emotional states are created by our sixth sense, our mind. There is permanent interaction between our mind's activity and the centres that rule our emotions. By stimulating the hypothalamus, and through the hypothalamus our autonomic nervous system and hormonal activity, our mind's imagination and fantasies can create an infinite variety of emotional states. Hearing a name, the news, noises, a telephone or door bell ringing, our imagination can create a change in the balance between sympathetic and parasympathetic systems, a different flow of hormones, a new emotional arousal.

Many emotional states can be detected through specific physical signs and the biological reactions they provoke. Some of these reactions are reflected facially, some in our eyes, some in bodily attitudes, some in gesticulations, and some in tones of voices. Most animals emanate a variety of scents, each of them corresponding to a specific emotional state. The predator, for example, will scent out the most nervous individual of the pack that it is chasing, and go for it. The smell released by a highly vulnerable animal is easily perceived by the alert senses of a hungry predator. Odours emanated by the females of many species when sexually aroused, play an essential part in their reproduction.

The inter-specific fights among animals are seldom mortal because of their accurate reading of the external signs of their emotional arousals.

Emotional signs become symbols for those who perceive them, for those who understand their meanings.

Before the development of the mind, relations among our

ancestors, and between them and other animals, were mainly ruled by the interpretation and understanding of this natural language consisting of the biological external signs of the emotions. In that evolutionary phase, in that pre-Babel period, our ancestors must have had a natural language common to the whole species. We read in Genesis: 'The whole earth was of one language and one speech.'

With the development of the mind's created fears, we developed a new series of emotions, emotions created by psychosomatic arousals, which started being expressed mainly vocally, slowly developing into speech. With its increased activity, the brain provided grammar and syntax, helping the speech to express these newly developed emotional arousals.

There is a tendency to place the centres of speech in certain areas of the brain. It must be stressed, however, that the energy needed for speech, as well as the energy that its inspiration and intonation need, are provided by emotional arousals. Many speech defects, as well as most forms of speechlessness, are mainly results of high emotional arousals. In fact, reducing emotional arousals by the de-dramatization of the mind's over-seriousness, a sense of humour can be the best medicine in curing speech defects.

A certain evidence that speech is intimately connected with emotional arousals can be deduced by the introduction of euphemisms.

From the beginning of the development of language, words and names used to describe frightening divinities, events, diseases or death, started being softened or sentimentalised. The main purpose of the euphemizing words or names associated with strong emotions was, and is still to-day, to appease the dreadful mysterious forces or magic powers they represented, or to placate the fears associated with them.

As humanity becomes more frightened as generations go by, languages become richer in their euphemisms. The general tendency to soften words and names with negative or unpleasant associations, has reached comic proportions at times. In order to endear the mother-in-law, the French call her 'la belle mère'. In order to reduce the fear of old age, the poetic term of 'the golden years' has been invented. Instead of using the word 'death', feared by so many, people say: 'They have passed away', or 'gone to higher service', for example.

As the mind's created feelings of vulnerability vary from individual to individual, so do the vocal and other expressions of the emotions caused by these feelings.

In spite of the continuous improvement in the vocabulary of our post-Babel era, speaking the same language and using the same words, we often create failures in communication and understanding. This is mainly due to the fact that we are still poor in verbal expressions, unable to convey the real meaning of the variety of our emotions and the even greater variety of their subtleties. These failures in communication and understanding seem to be here to stay, because we are getting richer in emotional states than in the vocabulary to express them. Often we experience emotional states that we have difficulty in expressing at all. The higher the emotional arousals, the less they are communicated by words, the more they are expressed by physical gestures or screams.

Individuals' differences in their emotional experiences contribute to their problems of communication and understanding. We can only understand others if we understand their emotions, and we can only understand their emotions if we experience, or if we have experienced similar emotions. Most of our tragedies, in fact, are a result of misunderstanding. Much of our communication is based on abstract speculation or guessing the meaning of others' words, attitudes or behaviour. Francis Bacon must have felt this when he stressed: 'Words still manifestly force understanding, throw everything into confusion, and lead mankind into vain and innumerable controversies and fallacies.'

With the development of the mind and its abstractly created values and fears, the human groups developed differences in their collective feelings of vulnerability, differences in their emotional arousals.

Influenced in their search for words by different living conditions, climate, local colours or environments, to express their emotions, these human groups developed different languages, and different dialects of the same language.

It is interesting to note that certain highly aggressive human groups have developed a variety of words to express killing, hitting or kicking, while few or no words to express gratitude or gentleness. In fact some languages adopted French 'merci' to express thank you.

How can a sense of humour help both our memory and our learning?

There can be no memorising or learning without emotional arousals created by feelings of vulnerability or fears.

As individuals of any other species, we have a natural optimal range of feelings of vulnerability and fears, a natural optimal range of balances between our sympathetic and parasympathetic systems, a natural optimal range of endocrine glands' activities. This optimal range of fears creates an optimal range of emotional arousals, and an optimal range of awareness, perceptiveness and learning.

In this optimal range, our awareness and perceptiveness are open to our internal milieu and to the external world in the most beneficial way for our survival and the survival of our species.

With these optimal emotional arousals we are fully open to learning, and our memory and learning are formed on objective reality. This enables us to adapt in the best way to the external world. It is, in this optimal range of emotional arousals that our common sense reasoning takes place.

Our natural optimal range of emotional arousals is, however, permanently inhibited by our mind's world. On one side lies the spectrum of decreasing emotional arousals, which limits our participation in real life, as our awareness and our perceptiveness diminish with the decrease of emotional arousals below their optimal level.

The spectrum of decreasing emotional arousals is mainly created by the mind's speculative and artificial reductions of our basic innate feelings of vulnerability and fears. Our mind is able to invent disinterest, complacency or resignation, all of which reduce the sympathetic system's activities below their optimal range, creating an insensitive or apathetic state of existence.

In order to reduce our inherited feelings of vulnerability and fears, our mind is also able to create a fictitious sense of safety or self-confidence. This can reduce our sensitivity to the point of callousness.

In advanced age we acquire a certain routine behaviour which reduces our basic feelings of vulnerability and fears, and which also diminishes our awareness and perceptiveness below their optimal range.

In the spectrum of low emotional arousals, memorisation and learning are superficial and of short duration. Events associated with a low emotional energy are either unable to encrust themselves on our brain, or they remain encrusted superficially for a relatively short period of time, thus creating a labile memory.

On the other side of the optimal range, there is a spectrum of the mind's created strong emotional arousals, a spectrum of balances between sympathetic and parasympathetic systems above their optimal range, and a spectrum of high activities of endocrine glands related to the sympathetic system. These strong emotional arousals are produced by an increase in our feelings of vulnerability and fears, mainly caused by escape from reality into the world of beliefs, ideologies and fantasies. Any escape into the fragile world of the mind's idealisations or pretentiousness increases fears.

There is another major source of stong emotional arousals. Any physiological disfunction of our autonomic nervous system, any irregularity in the activity of our hormonal glands, any biological pain or discomfort, creates a certain emotional state. Many conceited people can increase the intensity of their emotional arousals by becoming over-anxious about these physiological defects or disturbances. As I said before, a mind with an inflated ego is usually offended by physical discomfort or pain, and, when offended, the mind develops suffering or frustration.

The biological discomforts which occur to some during a full moon can produce high emotional arousals. A great part of our body being made up of water, we all, to some extent, feel a certain 'high tide' inside us during the full moon which creates tensions, uneasiness or discomfort. Many conceited people tend to over-dramatize their sensations, and this can bring them to states of high anxiety or depression.

Strong fears can be registered so deeply in our brain as to

become a structural part of it, and produce a permanently present excessive feeling of vulnerability, or inferiority.

With strong fears encrusted on our brain, our awareness and perceptiveness become chronically reduced.

A new information perceived in a precarious state of existence easily increases fears. This happens for the following reason. A mind in a state of precariousness, created by an escape into beliefs or fantasies, will only perceive information which flatters or encourages the existing beliefs or fantasies, thus increasing the precariousness of the world of beliefs or fantasies. When a fervent believer reads a book he will only perceive what is in accordance with his beliefs, and this takes him or her even further from reality. He will not register in his memory whatever is against his beliefs, as whatever is against his beliefs will increase his emotional arousal to the point of rage, to the point of imperceptiveness.

In certain states of high emotional arousals we feel threatened by everything. In these states we also start ruminating over our negative memories and thoughts. This merely perpetuates or worsens the anxiety and depression which are usually connected with strong emotional arousals.

Increasing the activity of their sympathetic system with their mind, therefore increasing their emotional arousals and decreasing the efficiency of their senses, some people succeed in becoming so insensitive that they can lie on a bed of nails, or walk on burning coal, without feeling pain.

Some of these high emotional arousals, coupled with the brain's release of its opiates, can create a state of elation, or an illusion of elevation or levitation.

Certain high emotional arousals, particularly those created by the strong beliefs of fervent fanatics can produce mystical experiences.

It is at certain levels of high emotional arousals that a sudden additional fear triggers off fits in epileptics. It is also that at certain levels of high emotional arousals an added fear drives people to suicide.

Exceptionally strong emotional arousals created by overpowering fears can cause panic, terror, trance or fainting, total insensitiveness and imperceptiveness.

One of the main biological purposes of the memory is to reduce the fears of the present and future in the light of past experiences. Past events can only alleviate or placate the fears of the present and future if created by the optimal range of emotional arousals, as only then do they represent real and useful experiences.

We fear the present and future whenever we look down at them from a static pedestal created by the mind.

Memories associated with strong emotional arousals are mainly rigid beliefs in a constant challenge of objective reality, and this creates tension and aggressiveness. A 'déjà vu' event, which in the optimal range of emotional arousals produces the calming effect of familiarity, in high emotional states is perceived as threatening.

In its self-deceit, the human mind creates the following absurdity. Those who escape from reality into a world of fantasies in order to achieve a fuller and more interesting life, reach the opposite of their hopes. In a refuge of fantasies we develop fear that the refuge may be derided or debased by reality, and this fear reduces our awareness and perceptiveness, thus limiting our participation in real life. The impression of safety that people sometimes develop in a refuge of fantasies or beliefs is mainly due to the reduced sensitivity produced by the fear carried by an escape or an exile.

In escaping from reality we escape time. In an escape, time is without duration; it is without duration because it is not filled with the experiences of life. Time registered in our memory consists of a vision of real experiences.

Periods of positive difficulties and deprivations last longer than the same lengths of time spent in comfort. The sense of reality imposed on us by positive difficulties and deprivations does not permit us to escape into the world of dreams and fantasies, it does not allow us to opt out of time and life.

With extra strong infatuations, time and life can even totally vanish.

By deriding the mind's artificial or speculative reductions or eliminations of our basic inherited feelings of vulnerability, a sense of humour can help us to eliminate the low emotional arousals and re-acquire the optimal ones.

By deflating our conceit and our mind's world of wishful beliefs and fantasies, a sense of humour can prevent us becoming dominated by strong fears. Helping us to remain in the optimal range of emotions, a sense of humour can keep us in contact with reality, and help us to learn about the positive world and real life. Strong emotional arousals push us towards only being interested in learning what will help us to escape further and further into unreality, into a world of bigger beliefs and fantasies.

Here, in fact, lies the human comedy brought about by our mind's ability for self-deception.

What is it that can help us in our escape into the world of beliefs and fantasies, and what is it that can help us to escape even further from the real world?

The one and only answer is: lies and deceptions. Lies and deceptions are the essential food of beliefs and fantasies.

One of the greatest propagators of the idealised world of the mind, Plato, openly stressed the positiveness of deceits. He called them 'useful lies'.

Escaping from the mind's created fears by means of lies and deceits, only increases fears, and this leads to a need for further lies and deceits, bringing stronger fears. People dominated by fears are like drug-addicts: the more they have them, the more they need them. No-one knows this better than demagogues of ideologies. They know that people in fear crave lies and deceits, and they provide them most generously with their false promises and propaganda.

We use our new brain and its vast creative abilities in order to produce fears, and then try to placate them with lies and deceits.

People living under regimes based on lies and deceits, have reached a curious absurdity: they learn ignorance, they learn how to evade the truth, they learn how to fool themselves. Those living in a world of beliefs tend to slip into even more fantastic fantasies. A believer's alternative to his beliefs is bigger beliefs.

The difference between genuine ignorance and learned ignorance is that, in its humbleness, the former is easily guided by intuitive common sense, while the latter becomes more and more seduced by ideology.

A large portion of humanity is, in fact, ruled by ideologies.

Where does an ideology find its seductive power and energy?

In fear of its enemy. An ideology cannot exist without an enemy. That is why leaders of ideologies create and cultivate a frightening devil, an evil monster which threatens their ideology and their lives, lives of lies and deceits. The seductive power of an ideology consists, therefore, in offering protection against an invented peril or enemy. If one peril or enemy disappears, the ideology invents another even more threatening peril, another even more frightening enemy.

An ideology also needs an enemy in order to have someone to blame for its failure to fulfill its Utopian promises. It is in the nature of an ideology to fail.

Without the West as its menacing evil, the Soviet bloc would disintegrate. Those who continue to hope for a peaceful co-existence between the West and Communism are unaware of the nature of an ideology.

An ideology also has to be at permanent war against its external enemies in order to eliminate its internal dissidents.

The hatred of the enemy of an ideology transforms people into prisoners of the leaders of that ideology. Hatred blinds, and the blind need guidance. Blinded by hatred, people automatically obey the orders of their authorities. A blind person finds his peace in obedience. In obedience lies his sense of belonging and protection. Coupled with the fears that dictatorships create, the politically useful cult of enemy and hate has brought an important negative consequence: a noticeable reduction in people's understanding, this essential condition of proper learning. The highly emotionally aroused only take in the language, behaviour and reasoning created by these high emotional arousals. They cannot understand the language, behaviour and common sense reasoning created by the optimal range of emotional arousals.

It is interesting to note that in the West only those who live in a certain state of high emotional arousals, mainly caused by their minds' created fears, usually produced by excessive personal pretentiousness, understand and practise the language, behaviour and reasoning of the Communist world. Communist fellow travellers in the West mainly come from the most vulnerable element, that of the so-called intellectuals. Many of these intellectuals live with the belief that they deserve more success and fame than they have achieved, and this creates strong and lasting fears, rage and hatred. I call these people pseudo-intellectuals because their academic learning does not serve their intelligence, but only their minds' beliefs and prejudices.

One of the main aims of Communist ideology is to create more and more of their fellow travellers by creating more and more frightened people in the West with their policy of constant and systematic menace.

People living under Communist dictatorships are, however, becoming gradually more and more immune to an ideological education.

A prolonged state of fear induced by Communist ideology, forces many people to escape into apathy, cynical detachment, resignation or withdrawal, into disinterest in learning and into poor memorising. At this stage, the authorities face a serious problem, that of alcoholism. Recently, Fjodor Uglov, a high ranking member of the Soviet Academy of Science, wrote in 'Isvestia': 'There are forty million alcoholics in the Soviet Union and one million die every year. One child in six is born with some kind of handicap caused by the drinking habits of one of the parents. The problem costs millions of lost production hours a year.'

There is only one thing that can bring these people back to life, and that is a sense of humour. But, a sense of humour is considered the greatest crime, the most sacrilegious of sins, by all ideologies.

A sense of humour could also help the aged, invalids and the chronically sick. Due to their diminished physical conditions, these people's fears increase, bringing them to emotional states which revive their most fearful memories. They can perceive events from their inner milieu and from the outside world in the most alarming way.

Those who survived Nazi extermination camps, or similar experiences, for example, could, in old age, start reviving the atrocities that happened, and therefore, suffer from high anxiety, insomnia and nightmares. In this gloomy state of existence, everything, from noise to colours, from news to names, reminded them of their dramatic past.

By creating a better 'umor', a more cheerful mood, a sense of humour could help revive more pleasant memories from the past.

In helping us to see the positive side of life today, a sense of humour builds up agreeable memories to be evoked in the future.

I would like to stress that, given the fact that our brain's mental activity, which ranges from rational intelligence to the irrational mind's fantasies, depending on the emotional arousals, educational systems should concentrate more on teaching us how to keep our emotional arousals inside their optimal range rather than to enrich our memory with facts, figures or ego appealing cultures. We all know that an illiterate peasant, whose constant contact with the laws and order of nature preserves him from becoming precious or pretentious, thus developing the mind and its fears, can be much happier and wiser than many university dons. Due to her cyclic physiology and her closer contact with the laws of nature, therefore less seduced by an 'ought to be' mind's ego, a woman is more inclined than a man to be guided by her brain's intelligence than by her brain's mind. Unfortunately a woman's common sense intelligence very often advises her to adapt to the fantasies of man's mind.

We tend to divide emotions and memories into the positive or negative, the exciting or depressing, the pleasant or unpleasant.

This classification is mainly determined by our mind. It is obvious that our mind will consider an emotional arousal as positive, exciting or pleasant, if events which created it gratify or delight our ego, or if they contribute to our ego's importance or value. We like things and persons involved in those events which please our mind's world. If the events or circumstances which provoked the same intensity of an emotional arousal were dmaging or displeasing to our ego, our mind would consider that arousal as a negative, depressing or unpleasant emotion. We dislike things and persons associated with those events which degrade our inflated ego. The same volume of an emotional arousal can create excitement or irritation, love or hate, anger or delight, depending on our mind's reaction to the events which provoked the arousal.

A strong stimulation can easily result in physical discomfort or pain. We are able, however, to consider physical discomfort, pain or self-inflicted torture, as positive emotions if they contribute to our aesthetic, or if they increase our sense of importance, dignity or vanity.

'Men ought to know,' Hippocrates stressed back in the fifth century B.C., 'that from the brain only arises our pleasures, joys, laughter and jests, as well as our sorrows, pains, griefs and tears.'

A sense of humour could shake this dualistic division of emotions by introducing a third: ridiculous emotions. Excessive emotions of the dualistic division could enter into this group. An excessive positive, exciting or pleasant emotion can be as ridiculous as an excessive negative, depressing or unpleasant emotion. They are both ridiculous because they both damage our physical and above all our mental health. In fact, many mental disorders are the result of a strong mind's emotional arousals.

A sense of humour can help keep emotional arousals within their physically and mentally healthy optimal range.

Ever since the mental activity of the human brain started producing the mind, and ever since the mind started creating its self-made fears, most people have always been somehow seduced or enchanted by excessive emotional arousals caused by these fears, because a great deal of artistic creativity finds its origin and its energy in these excessive emotionl arousals.

Looking at art with a sense of humour, and considering artistic creations as comic or humourous, would be considered madness by most people. Later I will explain, however, that artistic creativity and creations can, in fact, be ridiculous. They can be ridiculous simply because they are often intimidating or threatening. They are intimidating or threatening because they are a product of excessive emotional arousals and fears. Being intimidating or threatening, artistic creations raise our fears and emotional arousals. We have been indoctrinated by our culture to consider emotional arousals caused by the fear of artistic creations, as a positive excitement or an enjoyment.

We use all kinds of stimulants in order to increase our energy and arousal. Stimulants imply intoxication. By poisoning or irritating our body, stimulants create an alarming state of existence in which our organism increases its energy and alertness. We often call this state ecitment, which a certain dose of stimulants can transform into agitation.

Increasing irritation, the abuse of stimulants increases fear which limits alertness, sense/perception and mental activity. Excessive abuse of stimulants can drive people to escape into total apathy.

HUMOUR AS MEDICINE

Many hospitals have a depressing atmosphere which is largely due to the over-serious attitude of most doctors. Reflecting the adolescent mentality, physicians feel that their serious gloomy manner will impress the patients. They seldom realise that sick people are like frightened children, craving togetherness, intimacy and the light touch. They would help themselves, and particularly their patients, if they recalled the following words of Robert Burton: 'Humour purges the blood, making the body young, lively, and fit for any manner of employment.'

'Doctors are three times as likely to commit suicide than the average person, far more likely to be killed in an accident and many more times more likely to suffer mental breakdowns, alcoholism or drug addiction,' we read in a British survey. This must be due to the strenuous effort employed by physicians in performing their role of over-seriousness among the sick and the dying.

Doctors and nurses should be trained in the practice of humour. By treating people in a humourous and playful way, they could help their patients to reach a state of playfulness and youthfulness, both of which have great recovery potential. Swift was right when he said that: 'The best doctors in the world are "Dr. Diet", "Dr. Quiet" and "Dr. Merryman".' Centuries earlier, the famous Salernitan Medical School advised similar cures for a healthy life; 'Mens laeta, requies, moderata diaeta', meaning cheerfulness, quietude and a moderate diet.

The Bible gave the following advice: 'A merry heart doeth good like a medicine.'

Hippocrates, one of the first known physicians, advised the medical element to present a gay and radiant expression in front of their patients.

Throughout the world, patients would benefit if visits from priests, who, like vultures, remind people of Extreme Unction and death, were replaced by visits from humourists, comedians, jokers or merely happy children.

All in all, cheerfulness, playfulness and lightheartedness employed by nursing staff, would do far more good than any other medicine.

Humour could play an important role in modern medicine because of the increasing number of psychosomatic diseases. The most common of these dieseases are: migraine, allergies, high blood pressure, stomach ulcers, rheumatism, anorexia nervosa, skin rashes and diarrhoea.

In fact, if we take into consideration that psychosomatic diseases are mainly caused by the mind's self-created fears and worries, then humour is the best therapy for these afflictions. What is more, it is a therapy with positive side effects. Perhaps, psychosomatic diseases would be understood better if only medical science would take the trouble to delve deeper into the influences of our wishful thinking and our self-inflated ego on the glandular activity of our brain.

Excessive aspirations, pretentions, eagerness and avidity create uncertainty and apprehension which triggers off the hypothalamo-neuro-endocrine mechanism. This sustained sympathetico-adrenal activity creates a lasting emergency readiness causing prolonged strain on our body. Under this prolonged strain the 'locus minoris resistentiae', or the weakest organ, collapses, diminishing or breaking down the activity of our organism. Like a mechanical system or chain, our body breaks down with the erosion of the weakest link.

As each individual has its own 'focus minoris resistentiae', psychosomatic diseases vary from person to person. Under a similar strain, two individuals may develop different psychosomatic diseases.

What is more, when a psychosomatic disease is signalled to the cerebral cortex, it can open the way to worry, which, increasing the sympathetico-adrenal activity, worsens the situation.

In some cases this worry can trigger off the release of certain special neuro-transmitters which, stimulating the centre of the appetite in the hypothalamus, can develop a lasting hunger, an obesity, with all its negative consequences.

Many complain that their cause of stress is 'boring work'. Work is only boring when it is an effort. Work is only an effort when we consider it, or its environment, beneath our dignity, below our self-inflated self. That is when the motto of 'I don't like it', sets in.

In times of high unemployment, however the adolescent mentality find work less 'boring'. Perhaps this is because they have satisfied their conceit with having actually found a job at all.

Some people claim that the rat-race of modern life causes stress. But let us not forget that modern life has also provided extreme comforts. Maybe it is these very comforts and easy facilities which have increased our pretentions, thereby leading to stress and psychosomatic diseases.

There is a certain element that blame their bank over-drafts for their stress. The very idea of over-drafts could only have been inspired by minds that considered themselves entitled to live above their means.

Is cancer a psychosomatic disease? Could it be prevented or cured by humour?

I would like to explain the link between psychosomatic arousal, therefore emotional stress, and cancer.

As I have pointed out, the mind's created arousal is produced by an extra secretion of neuro-transmitters of the sympathetic nervous system and the extra secretion of the adrenal glands hormones. These neuro-transmitters and adrenal hormones stimulate a specific chain of our body's cells, increasing their activity above the normal. This over-activity of some of our body's cells goes at the expense of the activity of the many other cells and organs of our organism. Among the cells and organs whose activity is inhibited by the mind's created arousal are those dealing with our immune system. Any increase in the secretion of adrenal glands' hormones decreases the efficiency of existing white cells, whose normal role is to eliminate developing cancer cells. In an over-strained body there is decreased efficiency of its defensive system, a disruption of its self-monitoring capacity, and a depression in the formation and activity of antibodies. Reduced efficiency of the immune mechanism exposes us, some more than others, to all manners of infections, allergies and to the various types of cancer.

A healthy and efficient immune system easily recognises the abnormality of cancer cells, and either eliminates them or inhibits their reproduction. There is evidence that our immune system, even if unable to eliminate the newly formed cancer cells, can slow up or stem their dissemination.

We may all carry some form of cancer. Many people never develop it because their inner balancing system and immunity prevent it. Some people never discover that they have had cancer because it was arrested by natural defence.

It is established that cancer can be caused by viruses, chemicals or radiation. In order to start their pathological changes in a cell, these causes must find a cell that is receptive or ready for them. This readiness is provided by poor immunity and defence.

That reduced immunological efficiency of an organism can provoke cancer, or help the propagation of an existing one, can be deduced by the fact that the use of immuno-suppressive drugs can develop a new cancer, or disseminate an existing one. More than twenty percent of the people with an auto-immune disease, a disease of the immune system, develop some kind of cancer.

If there are indications that the danger of cancer increases with the decrease of the efficiency of the immune mechanism, and if there is positive evidence that the mind's created arousal is damaging our body's defences, and if there is proof that the mind's created emotional arousals, thus anxiety and stress, are caused by eager, avid or pretentious minds, then it is obvious that humour, which is able to reduce the mind's eagerness, avidity or pretentiousness, could help in preventing or curing cancer, or at least help the orthodox methods of preventing and curing it.

It is well known that hormonal imbalance plays an impotant part in the development of breast cancer. This imabalance is often caused, however, by the mind's created fears, and these can easily be eliminated by humour.

The sustained created emotional arousal of the mind also reduces the efficiency of our automatic mechanism for repairing the damaged cells. In an over-strained body, the repair system, which normally mobilises specialised enzymes to repair damage, slows down, becoming less efficient. Unrepaired damage of the genetic code-book of a cell can transform the cell into a malignant one. The importance of the automatic repair mechanism can be visualised better when we take into consideration the constant need for repair in a body since the structure of a living cell is permanently breaking down.

Some people may query the role played by the mind in the development and dissemination of cancer, by pointing out that animals and plants, with no mind, still develop cancer. Animals and plants can be victims of stress caused by environmental, climatic or cosmic abnormal conditions. Humans have the unfortunate privilege of not only developing stress due to abnormal external conditions, but also of creating it with their pretentious minds.

By using humour as therapy, or as an aid to conventional cancer treatment, patients would have nothing to lose but their worries, or at least a part of them.

Later on I will try to explain how to acquire a better sense of humour. Now, however, I would like to give some advice to those suffering from cancer, and to those trying to prevent it.

Those who have cancer, and above all those who want to prevent it, should use the idea of cancer as the best excuse to eliminate their rat-race life-style, their eagerness, avidity and pretentiousness. One should use the idea of cancer as an excuse to start living life, to start enjoying life. Most people spend their entire lives performing a self-imposed strenuous role, devouring themselves with their over-ambitions. Performing a role means assuming a false identity. Living with a false identity is like travelling with a forged passport. It is a life of fear and anxiety, and fear and anxiety are often the main causes of many forms of cancer. The best way to improve the efficiency of our immune system and of our automatic repair mechanism, and therefore our chances of preventing or curing a cancer, would be to withdraw from the 'stage' into an environment where one can rid oneself of masks, poses, affectations and pretentions. The obvious place for this type of retirement would be a happy family. Widening our reasoning, a sense of humour helps us to have a happy family. With intelligent reasoning we would work for a happy family before we actually needed it. Our immune mechanism and our automatic repair system, are in better shape when we belong to a group, when we are integrated.

There is evidence that many cancer patients, particularly those of a certain age, have recently lost their partner or closest friend. This is where a sad truth must be faced: those with the so-called 'broken heart syndrome' are those who selfishly leant on their lost partner or friend all their lives. In reality they have not got a broken heart but an increased fear of life. The 'broken heart syndrome' is hard to cure, but easily prevented. People should be taught that the best relationships are those which we create at our own expense, with our own generosity and understanding. Generosity and understanding quickly replace a lost partner or a lost friend.

For those who discover that acquiring a sense of humour is difficult, or for people who find that self-ridicule offends or degrades them, I advise the learning of gratitude. Surely, everyone can recall at least one happy time in their past on which to build the spirit of gratitude. There is one gratitude within everyone's reach, the gratitude of being alive, to have been born at all. Today's knowledge that conception is a miracle of chance and coincidence, should justify this. Much unhappiness and misery is caused by the fact that most people consider what they have to be their due. In the very name of these rights, we even strive for more, creating a life of permanent frustration. 'It is not the man who has little, but the man who craves more, that is poor,' as Seneca said.

Gratitude can have the same effect on the mind's eagerness, avidity and pretentiousness, and on emotional arousals and the anxiety and stress caused by them, as a sense of humour: the latter by deriding them, the former by smiling on them.

The thought that we might not exist at all or that we could be dead, should transform the idea of unfairness into luck. After all, whenever we fly, drive, or even cross the street, it could be for the last time. This should make us realise that life is a bonus, a constant gift, for which we should be grateful.

By playing with our mind's groundless assumption that we could do better, or have more, we unearth the thought that the opposite is also true. We could do worse, or have less, and there is much that could be worse in most people's lives. In a world ruled by uncertainty, 'worse' is a certain possibility. 'Tout peut toujours être pire', as Malraux said.

The realisation that things could be worse, opens the way to gratitude, and this helps us in eliminating the mind's created fears, anxiety and stress, thus preventing or helping to cure cancer, psychosomatic diseases and mental disorders.

We should always remember the following fact: our intelligence can be as powerful as our mind in psychosomatic relationships. Our mind is able to produce cancer, psychosomatic diseases and mental disorders. Our intelligent reasoning is able to create psychosomatic well-being and mental harmony.

With gratitude we also acquire the greatest gift: time. By smiling at the mind's eagerness, avidity and pretentiousness, we eliminate the mind's created fears. By eliminating these fears, we discover time, time to reason, time to understand, time to play, time to prevent diseases or to recover from them, time to laugh and time to live.

Providing time, gratitude creates a life of elegance and taste. Enabling us to make demands on ourselves, to give, time inspires nobility. Sophocles must have recognised this when he wrote: 'Time is a gentle deity.' What a difference with today's motto: 'Time is money.'

Those who think that gratitude might lower their status should be told that greatness can also be obtained through gratefulness.

Gratitude also immunises us against the poison spread by prophets of gloom and doom, and to intimidation by those who revel in making life sad and miserable.

Judeo-Christianity contributed much to gloom and doom. If

only Moses had introduced 'Thou shalt not take thyself too seriously,' as an Eleventh Commandment, our lives might have been happier and healthier. In fact, our culture produces more cancers, psychosomatic diseases and mental disorders than any other culture.

If Christ had died on the Cross with a smile of gratitude for having been chosen as the Son of God, perhaps people would have smiled more over the past two thousand years.

This self-imposed gloom and over-seriousness have gradually reached extremes in certain parts of our adolescent mentality's world. In some Western Capitalist countries a smile is considered a sign of frivolity, or of inadequate competitiveness. In Communist countries smiling is politically suspect. In Sweden, anyone caught smiling is in danger of being breathalised.

Unhappy or in fear of orthodox therapy, such as surgery, radiation and chemo-therapy, many cancer patients try what is known as 'alternative medicine'.

One of these 'alternative medicines' is the so-called 'imagery process' or 'healing visualisation'. This involves the patient mentally picturing the white blood cells of the immune system successfully fighting the cancer cells, several times a day; a kind of war between the goodies and the baddies.

Inspired by the idea of fighting an enemy, this 'imagery process' can sometimes increase the arousal and stress which were often the very cause of the cancer in the first place. The 'imagery process' could be used instead, however, to eliminate arousal by placating the mind's fears and worries. This might help the body's immune system and its automatic repair mechanism.

Various 'nutritional therapies', based on the theory of 'potassium starvation' of modern man, pretend to be able to prevent and even to cure cancer. Nutritional therapy could be advantageous if it was coupled with humour therapy. The right diet cannot eliminate the mind's created arousal, and this arousal, as well as having other negative effects on the body, often inhibits digestion of even the most sensible food. A lasting mind's created arousal can also diminish the efficiency of the insulin secreting glands, which in turn diminishes the metabolism of carbohydrates.

Some unorthodox methods for the treatment of cancer insist that by 'creating within an individual the will to live and the feeling that there is something to fight for might result in a reversal of the stress situation.' Supporters of this method fail to take into consideration that 'the feeling that there is something to fight for' merely creates more arousal and stress. They make the mistake of considering arousal as a sign of vitality. The mind's created arousal, with its agitation, restlessness or aggression, on the contrary, reduces vitality.

There is a further danger in 'alternative medicine'. Patients using an 'alternative medicine' can easily develop a feeling of righteousness which, being a precarious state, increases the mind's created arousal.

Due to strokes, kidney failure and major surgery in which parts of the body have been extracted, there are an increasing number of invalids today. These people have a particular need to laugh at themselves. Using humour-therapy in re-habilitation would help this. No invalid happily adapts himself to his changed life without a sense of humour.

These people need a sense of humour above all for the following reason. An invalid is a dependent being. In a state of dependence, one revokes other states of dependence from the memory, and this brings sadness and depression.

Humour could be an effective cure for alcoholism. One way to apply this therapy would be to organise plays and farces in 'drying out' centres, ridiculing drunks. Performing the role of a drunk when sober, might de-dramatise the state of mind which drove the alcoholics to the bottle in the first place.

A similar therapy could be applied to drug-addicts, who are in even greater need of de-dramatisation to be able to perceive reality more clearly and acquire a sounder reasoning.

A sense of humour could also help us to help ourselves.

At the first sign of a problem in our physical or mental health, we rush for professional aid. This invites over-medication with its dangerous side-effects. Dependence on professional experts destroys the capacity for self-help.

Ageing gracefully should be one of the aims of life.

If people agreed on this, then they should be more interested in humour and its potential in immuno-therapy. There is positive evidence that the negative sides of ageing are mainly due to the progressive inefficiency of our immune system. In fact, ageing is preceded by a reduction in the efficiency of the thymus and the spleen, important organs of the defence mechanism. It is interesting to note that people in ancient times used to place the source of laughter in the spleen. Perhaps nowadays, laughter inspired by a sense of humour could enhance the activity of this organ.

Being capable of eliminating the over-strain on our organism, a sense of humour can also improve our automatic repair mechanism. Any reduction in the efficiency of this mechanism, increases ageing and the negative aspects of it.

Using a sense of humour reasoning, we can reduce the mind's fears or worries caused by physical pain. Eliminating emotional arousals caused by these fears or worries, a sense of humour reasoning alleviates the body's tension and strain. As I said before, any tension or strain, caused by an emotional arousal, irritates, stresses or stretches bodily damages, thus increasing the painfulness of physical pain.

A humour therapy could be a great help to those suffering from allergies.

In order to have allergies one usually has to be open to them, to be in a state of irritability, or to have part of one's body in a state of abnormal excitability. External elements such as certain food, pollens, or the presence of dogs or cats can only irritate us if we are in a state of irritability, if we are open to their harmful effects. Irritability or excitability, which are the real causes of allergies, are normally created by tension or stress, originated by emotional arousals, produced by a state of precariousness, which is usually generated by the mind's escape into some kind of exaggerated self-centredness or self-concern. In fact, when people are in a good mood, joyful spirit, or pleased in their egos, they are seldom irritated by elements or situations which in a state of anxiety and stress give them allergies.

Liberating the mind of its self-created state of precariousness or worries, a humour therapy, based on the derision of our exaggerated self-centredness and self-concern could be more beneficiary, and cheaper, in freeing us from allergies than present cures.

Humour could help in preventing the crippling and widely spreading disease of rheumatoid arthritis.

Before attacking the joints, most forms of arthritis start as an inflammation of the soft tissues connected with the joints.

Inflammatory agents have an easier task if these tissues are in a receptive condition.

Tension, strain, stress and stiffness, caused by emotional arousals created by the mind's fears, worries or sufferings, make these connective tissues more susceptible to inflammation, and also to the spreading of it once triggered off. It is known that the loss of a loved-one or even a job, can revive a latent arthritis or start a new one. In fact, some doctors prescribe tranquillizers to those afflicted by this disease.

That the mind plays an important part in the development of arthritis and other forms of rheumatism can be deduced by the fact that these diseases have increased with the advancement of civilization and progress. Perhaps this can be explained by pointing out that with the advance of civilization and progress people's pretentiousness and expectations increase, which mean disappointments and disillusions, causing emotional arousals, therefore tension, strain, stress or stiffness of the connective tissues, originated by the mind's fears, worries or sufferings.

It is interesting to note that many people afflicted with arthritis or other forms of rheumatic diseases suffer from an allergy.

Being capable of eliminating the causes of tension, strain, stress or stiffness, humour enables the connective tissues to become more resistent to inflammation, and prevent those existing to spread to the joints, by which time the chances of curing the arthritis become more limited.

Present drugs for arthritis can only alleviate the pain. They seldom change the course of the disease.

Humour has another advantage on drugs: it has positive side-effects.

I would like to end this chapter by mentioning that experiments carried out at the Common Cold Research Unit in Salisbury, England, show that over-serious and gloomy people are far more susceptible to ordinary colds than the cheerful ones.

HUMOUR AND MENTAL DISORDERS

There is much confusion in the field of mental disorders. This is mainly due to the fact that the professionals who deal with our psyche, perceive humanity through a personal screen of speculative theories, and usually try to force reality to suit their apprioristic opinions. Through his patient, a psychiatrist generally tries to achieve his self-assertion. By slotting his patient into one of his theories, he tries to fulfill himself.

The confusion in the field of mental disorder is worsening because of the increasing tendency of modern psychiatry to be more and more interested in creating mental disorders, than in their cure. One has the impression that the professionals dealing with mentally disturbed people want more and more people under their spell.

In my view, mental disorders mainly belong to adolescence: they start with its development, and are perpetuated by the adolescent mentality in other ages, including old age.

There is nothing physically wrong with the brain of mentally disturbed people. Mental disorders are simply a result of the reduced mental activity of a physically normal brain. As I said before, each individual has his optimal range of emotional arousals. During this range, the mental activity of the brain usually results in common sense intelligent reasoning and behaviour. Most mind-created emotional arousals are beyond this optimal range. In higher emotional arousals, the mental activity of our brain becomes restricted, thus producing a partial, incomplete, rough, incoherent, or inappropriate way of thinking and behaviour. This reduced activity of the brain, with its inferior, unusual or bizarre way of thinking and behaving, is what is known as mental disorder.

During exceptionally high emotional arousals, caused by terror, for example, the mental activity of the brain can completely disappear.

The intensity of mental disorders varies in relation to the intensity of the mind's created fears. These fears are usually originated by the escape of an adolescent ego from reality, into a world of fantasies and dreams. One could stress, therefore, that behind any mental disorder lies an inflated ego living dangerously in fear of failure. The more inflated an ego, the more unusual and abnormal the mental activity of its brain becomes.

Our brain's mental activity is reduced or restricted during high emotional arousals because the flow of blood to the brain, diminishes. High emotional arousals are created by emergencies, and in emergencies the blood concentrates on the organs specialised in emergencies, organs which provide the physical actions of fighting, flight or hiding.

High emotional arousals also inhibit the activity and efficiency of the sensory system and perceptive mechanism, which contribute to the distortion and abnormality of the brain's mental activity.

It should be stressed that the brain of mentally disturbed people is able to reason most normally and intelligently when operating inside the optimal range of emotional arousals. This is why I would like to point out once again that schools, particularly those dealing with the adolescent age, should introduce courses on how to keep fears and emotional arousals within their optimal range.

Science usually explains that some of the following symptoms are connected with mental disorders: anxiety, melancholia and pessimism, irritability, intolerance, loss of appetite and sexual potency, insomnia, high blood pressure, palpitations, over-breathing, sweating, pallor, inquietitude, dizziness, malaise, disorientation, aches, pains, skin rashes, insensitivity to the problems of others, lack of sympathy or humaneness, lack of consideration or understanding, lack of sense of humour or gratitude, lack of flexibility and adaptability and a reduced efficiency of sense-perception.

But these are not symptoms of mental disorders: they are the results of neuro-endocrine activity during the strong mind's created fears.

Being able to shake the mind's fears, a sense of humour can help in many mental disorders. After all, mental disorders entitle us to take them humourously. Most mental disorders are, in fact, theatrical and funny. Most of them are either farcical self-importance or melodramatic self-love; either a grotesque self-aggrandisement or a tragic self-infatuation; either a pantomime of self-exaltation or a charicature of self-admiration.

In our adolescent way of reasoning we seldom dare laugh at mental disorders because we see in them our hidden selves.

By taking ourselves too seriously, we often create or encourage mental disorders in others. Many eccentrics, aiming at creating a playful or joyful atmosphere, or inspired by naive 'attention seeking', have been transformed into mental cases. By facing them with over-seriousness, we often frighten them, pushing them to excess. We face eccentricities with over-seriousness because we are frightened that they may shake our self-importance. Strong believers are capable of persecuting or prosecuting eccentrics.

Many people claim that most mental dissorders stem from 'failure of adaptation.'

With a sense of humour reasoning, it might be found that the failure to adapt is in reality the failure of the self-fulfillment of a selfish and self-centered individual, the failure of the self-asserting strategy of a self-opinionated ego.

In our adolescent way of thinking, we consider that each individual is entitled by some sacred right, to excessive self-love, to an unscrupulous self-centredness, and to unlimited pretentiousness. What is more, each individual has a further sacred right: that of the fulfillment of his self-inflated self.

A sense of humour reasoning could recognise mental disorder as a dishonest game. In fact, a mentally disturbed person often tries to assert or fulfill himself beyond his merits. Any dishonest game deserves derision.

I would now like to mention some of the main neuroses and

psychoses, and try to explain that behind most of them lies an over pretentious mind.

A nervous breakdown usually hits those who sink into a state of hopelessness. A sense of hopelessness can only be reached with excessive hopefulness.

By developing a sense of self-ridicule, one can emerge from any hopeless situation.

Statistics show that single people are more liable to nervous breakdowns. Delving deeper, statistics might prove that single people are only single because of their selfishness and pretentiousness. Excessive selfishness and pretentiousness prevent communication, integration and togetherness. Personal sacrifices are essential for togetherness. Group or family life, built on personal sacrifices, is the best therapy in preventing nervous breakdowns or any other mental disorders.

Phobias are mainly developed by the fears which our mind creates when it escapes from reality into excessive self-importance. In analysing agoraphobia, I hope to make my theory clearer.

People suffering from agoraphobia explain that they fear public places. This fear is secondary to an agoraphobic's main fear, the fear created by his escape into an exaggerated self-importance. It is really that he does not dare face public places in case people might deride him by lowering him from his assumed pedestal.

Self-derision could placate an agoraphobic's panic because it would eliminate his emotional arousal, thus reducing the dizziness and over-breathing which are the main cause of his panic.

Behind kleptomania, for instance, there usually lies an excessive degree of self-righteousness, which, like any other self-made abstraction, can be shaken or eliminated by a sense of humour or self-derision.

Psychiatry explains that hysteria is a 'body language', a reaction to stress caused by an 'intolerable life situation'.

Obviously we place ourselves in an intolerable life situation whenever our pretentious ego does not match up to the capabilities of our real self.

In ancient times, people believed that hysteria was the result of demonic possession. They were partially right. In fact, our world of the mind's fantasies and dreams is full of demons. Dostoevsky described the possessive power of abstract ideas in many of his works.

In certain cases of hysteria, the vision, smell, taste or hearing are reduced. This is not due to the hysteria, however, but to the emotional arousal created by fear which an ego's escape into self-preciousness originates. This emotional arousal can also provoke hysterical vomiting or other problems of the digestive system.

The playful teasing of an hysterical person's self-preciousness could be a great help to this particular problem. In fact, hysterics crave playing. It is often this lack of play which created their longing for attention in the first place.

Hypochondriasis is mainly caused by excessive self-concern, inspired by an exaggerated idea of self-appreciation. Humour and playful teasing could replace the mirror that a hypochondriac carries in front of him, with an open window to the external world.

'Depression is suffered by people who see no reason to like themselves at all' ...'Depression is a state of self-hate,' wrote an English authoress, who ended her own life in a moment of depression.

What kind of people 'see no reason to like themselves at all'?

Those who develop a feeling of worthlessness, a feeling which is reached whenever we realise we are unable to achieve our ideals or aspirations. We can never achieve our ideals or aspirations if they are inspired by an excessive idea of self-admiration.

We only feel sorry for ourselves when we develop exaggerated self-adulation.

We develop 'self-hate' when we are disillusioned by self-love, and we are bound to be disillusioned by self-love if we stretch it too far.

The best cure for depression would be to reduce the ideals or aspirations that are beyond our ability to achieve them. The obvious way to lower our ideals or aspirations would be to play with our idea of self-admiration, to take it humourously.

The feeling of worthlessness can easily be cured by feeling

needed, and we can all be needed by reducing our sense of self-admiration. Happy are those who love people who need them; unhappy are those who love people they need.

Fears created by an escape into self-adulation create high emotional arousals which evoke from the memory mainly negative, chaotic or annihilating events in a depressive person, and this contributes to transforming his life into a life of threatening darkness, and his dreams into nightmares.

Living in a highly precarious state, a depressive's ego is sensitive to the smallest, even non-existent threats. Some people with especially over-developed self-admiration can acquire depression with a common cold, or barely significant damage or disequilibrium in their bodies.

As I explained before, some people develop depression during a full moon. Their excessive fears or worries about their biological uneasiness, due to disharmony in their water metabolism, and to the increases in hydrostatic and osmotic pressures, generated by the 'tidal wave' caused by the gravitational pull of the full moon over the bodies' water, stimulate the activities of the sympathetic nervous system and the adrenal glands. These activities create emotional arousals, tension and stress which create the symptoms of depression.

Being able to shorten the gap between the self-inflated ego and the real self, a sense of humour can help depressives to reduce their problems by limiting their egos' conceits. The ancients were more accurate in their approach to depression. It was considered a sin, and was cured by prayer. In fact, excessive self-adulation is more of a sin than a disease.

About half the prescriptions doled out in Western countries are for tranquillizers, anti-depressants or sleeping pills. This is mainly due to the fact that affluence and comfort often increase conceit and pretentiousness, both of which carry anxiety and stress.

Western culture's cult of the individual, of its independence and aggressiveness, creates a frightening loneliness in which depression and other mental disorders prosper.

During the menopause, many women develop some of the following: hot flushes, sudden heavy sweating, insomnia, agitation, palpitations, headaches, backache, loss of self-confidence, nervous breakdowns, melancholia and depression. Medical science explains that these problems are largely caused by the physical changes realised by the reduced production of the hormones, oestrogen and progesterone in the body.

But is this really the case?

Why do so many women hardly notice their menopause? Some even welcome it as an end to their messy and handicapping monthly periods. What is more, why, in their mid-life crises, without any change in their hormonal levels, do men acquire many female menopausal problems?

In my opinion, the answer to these questions lie in the fact that both the female menopause and the male mid-life crisis have the same origin: the human mind, or to be more precise, the adolescent mind's fear of ageing triggered off by an over-dramatisation of the first signs of physical change.

This fear of ageing creates an emotional arousal, therefore, an anxiety, tension or stress which provokes the above mentioned menopausal or mid-life crises' problems.

What is more, this fear of ageing significantly reduces man's sexual virility, this pride of the adolescent-minded, which only aggravates the problems.

One can see the validity of my theory by the fact that the stronger the adolescent characteristics, such as selfishness, self-centredness, and pretentiousness, in both men and women, the more acute their crises will be when faced with the first signs of ageing. For them these signs are a terrible shock, the end of their mind's illusions, the end of an era, an era in which their egos were the centre of the Universe. Middle-age does not create problems in mature-minded men or women, it creates problems for the adolescent-minded who fear maturing, as maturing means climbing down from the infatuation of the mind's world, into reality.

More dependent on their inflated egos than women, men are far more vulnerable during their mid-life crisis than women during the menopause. Most men try desperately to escape from the fear of ageing: some find refuge in alcohol or drugs, some try to solve their problem by running off with young secretaries or airhostesses, some by chasing after young girls or young men, whatever the case may be, in order to prove themselves still virile. Some resort to religious or ideological fanaticism, some to suicide, some become obsessed with health and physical fitness by dieting and jogging, some try to solve their problem with divorce, some start dressing in young or trendy styles, some try to revive the gang life, some homosexuals turn to heterosexualism, and some heterosexuals to the 'gay' life.

There is positive evidence that men and women who have a sense of humour, who do not over-dramatise their ageing, who do not take themselves over-seriously, or consider themselves the centre of the Universe, do not have menopausal or mid-life crises.

A sense of humour, in fact, could help a lot in placating the fear of ageing because it implies maturing, and maturing faces ageing with serenity. The problems of the female and male menopause are psychosomatic disorders created by pretentious and conceited minds, and a pretentious and conceited mind is the source of ridicule.

In order to induce the adolescent minded to face their mid-life crises less dramatically, I would like to point out that in maturity and serenity, sex and the pleasure connected with it, can increase, as in maturity one becomes more relaxed and more giving, thus helping to achieve true intimacy. 'Worries are the death of sexual potency,' as an Italian proverb goes.

Instead of complaining, the middle-aged should look forward to the best years of their lives. This could be achieved if they kept in mind that old age is a bonus, that one hundred years ago, and in many under-developed countries today, life expectancy was, and is, before middle-age.

Reaching middle-age, people should be grateful for continuing to live beyond their reproductive age, to survive their biological necessity. Jung stressed that there was no need for the sake of our species to live beyond forty years.

Perhaps, the flushes that some women experience during their mid-life crises, are really blushing with embarrassment for not being grateful for their bonuses in life. If this is the case, gratitude is the answer to their problems.

Following today's attitude of psychiatry, a psychosis is the result of a maladjusted person's escape from a hostile and uncooperative external world.

The maladjustment of a paranoic is not caused by a hostile and uncooperative world, but by shattered expectations, expectations inspired by ideas of grandiosity. A paranoic does not escape from reality, but from a world of his own frustrated illusions into a world of other bigger and deeper illusions. This only increases his emotional arousal, which leads him towards delusions. Delusions are the result of the brain's activity under certain high emotional arousals created by fears of escape into illusions. Being populated by all kinds of imaginary enemies, the paranoic's world of delusions, this extreme escape of the human mind, is a world of fears, and this perpetuates or increases the delusions.

Those dealing with a paranoiac's complaints should explain in a humourous way, that it is silly to be resentful that his friends or society in general will not permit him to have a grandiose life, based on excessive egomania, at their expense.

A paranoiac, in fact, fears teasing and derision because he knows that he is playing a selfish game at the expense of others. Proof that a paranoiac is trying to fool others, is that he fears their contempt even more than their teasing or derision. He fears contempt because of the dishonesty of his game. That he knows his game is unfair can be deduced from the fact that he is often afraid of being cheated.

Persecution mania is the result of suspicion. Suspicion, however, is caused by the fear of being suspected, and the fear of being suspected is caused by a secret. The secret of a paranoiac is his game in which he tries to enslave his environment to his grandiosity in which selfishness and self-centredness have reached extremes.

High emotional arousals, caused by precariousness produced by a paranoiac's escape into the world of illusions, inhibit the activity and efficiency of his sense-perception, which contributes to his misunderstanding or mis-interpretation of the external world.

Most schizophrenics are the victims of their excessive self-infatuation. Failing to find a life to suit his pretentiousness in the external world, a schizophrenic escapes into an imaginary superiority. This escape develops deep fears and high emotional arousals. Under these arousals, a schizophrenic's mental activity is reduced to a disorderly way of thinking and hallucinations. Some extra strong fears created by an escape into omnipotence or majesty can become paralysing which is often reflected in a schizophrenic's statuesque rigidity and immobility.

A schizophrenic's split personality is a result of his two ways of thinking, the two ways of his brain's mental activity: one under the optimal or near optimal range of emotional arousals, the other under the range of high emotional arousals.

During these high emotional arousals, a schizophrenic's sensory system and perception become strongly inhibited, and this contributes to his distorted way of thinking and hallucinations.

Latest research is trying to develop a diagnostic test for schizophrenia through the defects of patients' speech. There is, in fact, an important connection between the two: they are both the results of high emotional arousals caused by strong fears. During these high emotional arousals both the brain's contracted or shrunken mental activity, and a restricted linguistic fluency or a weakened speech's accuracy take place.

Some experts explain that today's impersonal city life leads more and more people towards schizophrenia. Could it not be that material progress, better living conditions, labour-saving gadgets of modern civilization, consumption on credit (therefore above our means), and city life, flatter an individual's mind to the point of such conceit and self-esteem, that it creates extreme isolation and loneliness? It is far easier to develop conceit in a large city than in a small village. In a village, conceit is quickly derided. In the city we can easily avoid contact with others because others try to avoid us in order to protect their own fantasies about themselves.

Many psychiatrists claim that the best way to cure a schizophrenic is to try and restore his 'self-esteem', lost in his 'maladaptation'. A schizophrenic does not lack self-esteem; on the contrary, he has an excess of it, and the proof is his total lack of humility.

In the forties and fifties there was a certain fashion and conviction that violent mental disorders could be cured with lobotomy or psycho-surgery. Parts of the frontal lobe of the neocortex, where volition and wishfulness were supposed to take place, were destroyed or their connection cut off from the rest of the brain. In my view, it would be more reliable, apart from being cheaper, and safer to try and inhibit the parts of the brain dealing with volition and wishfulness with humour instead.

Today schizophrenia is mainly treated with what are considered strong tranquillizers. Many, however, whether curing or being cured, worry about the side effects of these drugs.

Are what we call the side effects of antipsychotic drugs really due to these drugs?

In my view, these antipsychotic drugs do not reduce or eliminate the high emotional arousals which cause schizophrenia, but only partially succeed in reducing or inhibiting the influence of high emotional arousals on the brain's mental activity. In fact, antischizophrenic drugs diminish, sometimes significantly, a schizophrenic's disorderly thinking, hallucinations, paranoid ideations, grandiosity, hostility or belligerence.

In spite of their beneficiary effect on the brain's mental activity, these drugs do not affect a schizophrenic's emotional arousals. These arousals continue to exercise their negative effects on a schizophrenic's body.

The so-called side effects of antipsychotic drugs consist of one or more of the following symptoms: insecurity, restlessness, sleeplessness, sweating, palpitations, tremors, spasms, significant reduction of sexual interests in both sexes, and irregularity or cessation of menstrual cycles in women, dyskinesia, or impaired or abnormal motion of voluntary and involuntary muscles, difficulty in speech, social isolation, timorousness and suspicion.

All these so-called side effects of antischizophrenic drugs could in reality be results of emotional arousals created by the extra activities of the sympathetic nervous system and of the adrenal glands, produced by the mind's created fears or worries.

A sense of humour therapy could be a useful adjunct to the chemotherapy of the schizophrenia, as it could at least partially placate the mind's fears or worries that are unaffectted by antipsychotic drugs.

But these drugs do have a certain side effect: schizophrenics become dependent on their drugs. Dependence on drugs tend to lead to social withdrawal, preventing the so needed communication and close cooperative relationships. Perhaps a humour group therapy could solve this problem.

There is a tendency to attribute schizophrenia to inherited genes. Scientists claim that children with one schizophrenic parent have at least a ten percent risk of developing this mental disorder whether they live with their natural parents or with other people who are not affected by it.

I think that it should be taken into consideration that the possibility that childrren raised by a schizophrenic parent or parents become strongly susceptible to fears due to their parent's or parents' unusual or bizarre behaviour.

It should also be taken into consideration that the adopted children of schizophrenic parents run a greater risk of being schizophrenic, not so much because of inherited genes, but because they live in permanent precariousness and insecurity caused by the persecuting feeling that they were unwanted and abandoned by their natural parents. What is more, a foster parent is an acting parent, a performer of a role of a parent. An assumed role easily creates tension and stress in those who are performing the role and in those for whose sake the role is performed.

Many blame society for mental disorders. In my view, it would be better for the society, and above all to the mentally disturbed if the blame was concentrated on the true cause of mental disorders: the excessively inflated ego of the adolescent minded individuals.

All escapes from reality into beliefs, illusions or infatuations carry the fear of falling back to reality. These minds self-created fears, unique to the human species and then only in its adolescent mentality, produce a range of emotional arousals above their optimal levels. The higher these emotional arousals are, the more inadequate and reduced the brain's mental activities are. It is in these brains inadequate and reduced mental activities that mental disorders find their origin.

The inadequate and reduced brain's mental activity and the diminished efficiency of our sensory system and perceiving mechanism can best be seen in rushing. The fear of not being able to accomplish enough to please our pretentious ego creates emotional arousals which produce restlessness, agitation and rushing. These emotional arousals also produce a reduced mental activity and a diminished efficiency of the sense-perception. In fact, rushing is considered mad by any common sense reasoning.

Mental institutions are even gloomier than hospitals. There is often an atmosphere of hatred in these institutions, the staff hate the inmates, the inmates hate the staff, and the psychiatrists hate themselves for playing the fool among mad people.

The humourless psychiatrists and staff must be unaware that most of the inmates are there because they lack a sense of humour. Instead of treating these cases with playfulness, psychiatrists and their staff try to cure the patients with tragic over-seriousness.

In their role of over-seriousness, psychiatrists take psychiatry too seriously. This often removes them from reality to such an extent that they start to see madness in normal people. They pay for this over-seriousness and lack of humour, however. The suicide rate is even higher among psychiatrists than in any other branch of the medical profession.

Mental hospitals should organise classes on humour for the doctors and staff, as well as for the inmates. They should also show cartoons, comic films, and provide amusing literature, playgrounds, toys, swimming pools, gyms and particularly non-competitive physical exercise. Many mental patients are committed because they have been upset by competition.

A sense of humour also creates a certain familiarity, and familiarity can be a great help in the recovery of those who are mentally upset.

I would like to add that there is only one way of escaping a dramatic reality: by de-dramatising it. Any situation can be de-dramatised by mocking one's own pretentions and excessive expectations.

HUMOUR AND PREGNANCY

In his 'Quaderni', Leonardo da Vinci wrote the following about pregnancy: 'The same soul governs the two bodies ... the things desired by the mother are often found impressed on the child which the mother carries at the time of the desire ... one will, one supreme desire, one fear that a mother has, or mental pain has more power over the child than over the mother, since frequently the child loses its life thereby.'

Since then, no-one has said anything more about the interesting subject of embryogenesis.

During pregnancy, neuro-transmitters and hormones created in the mother's body by her fears or worries, and particularly by the more persistent ones, can pass into the embryo, influencing the development of its emotional centres and memory, and predisposing the progeny to the fears or worries which impressed the mother.

It is a myth that our happiest moments were those in utero. A child in utero is frequently bombarded by the fears caused by his mother's emotional arousals, which are more or less constant given the particular sensitivity of a mother during pregnancy.

Evidence that the mother's emotional arousals influence her embryo is the embryo's REM sleep. A child in utero spends a great deal of time moving his closed eyes.

What provides the energy for this activity?

In my view, it can only be supplied by the mother's fears. These fears stimulate the emotional centres in the child's brain. The stimulation of his emotional centres activates his visual cortex and his optic nerve which are directly connected with his emotional centres, and are responsible for eye movements during certain phases of sleep.

Only a mother's transmission of her fears can explain our instinctive or inherited fears. Many animals, as soon as they are born, carry in their memories, formed in their pre-natal phase of development, sound, smell, shape, movement or vision of their natural enemies or predators.

I think that we also inherit certain cultural or religious predispositions through our mothers' fears of taboos.

Our inherited fears can be seen in frequent REM sleep of neonates, the evident sign of higher activities of the sympathetic nervous system and of the adrenal glands. Being more frightened than full-time babies, prematures have more REM sleep. REM sleep fills approx. 80 percent of the total sleep of a ten week premature infant and approx. 65 percent of the time of infants born 2-4 weeks prematurely.

A mother's mental disorder can also be transmitted to her progeny. The high emotional arousals connected with her disorder can shape the child's emotional centres so that he becomes more than usually sensitive to certain fears.

Scientists have established that children of alcoholic mothers have more inclination to mental disorder than those whose mothers did not drink during pregnancy. I would like to suggest that these mental disorders are just as likely to be a consequence of the mother's fears or emotional stresses which drove her to the bottle, than of the alcohol itself.

Given the fact that many women are more worried during their first pregnancy than during subsequent ones, (presuming that they had no troubles), first born children incline to be more sensitive to fears than their younger brothers or sisters.

Those whose embryogenesis took place during a war or a revolution tend to be timid throughout their whole lives.

It would be intriguing to know if it is true that the K.G.B. infiltrate the Western media, regularly illustrating the consequences of a nuclear disaster, in order to influence pregnant women, thereby predisposing the next generation towards unilateral disarmament.

If there is clear evidence that a pregnant woman's negative feelings can create organically based emotional imbalance, psychological disorder, sexual and personality problems, or scar her offspring for life, then her positive feelings should create better adjusted children, a healthier humanity and people with far fewer physical and emotional problems.

I am sure that one of the major sciences of the future will be pre-natal psychology, as the experience of the embryo in the uterus shapes people's lives and personalities. I feel certain that a sense of humour will play an important part in this pre-natal psychology. Eliminating often unnecessary fears or worries, a sense of humour could contribute a great deal to a pregnant woman's serenity and maturity.

Fortunately for our species, however, many pregnant women acquire a sense of humour, a naturally mature way of reasoning, otherwise we would be even more neurotic and suicidal.

Forced to re-adapt themselves to the adolescent mentality and way of life, after childbirth many women go through serious emotional crises. Post-natal depression does not exist, however, in non-industrial societies, particularly those where native tradition or age-old established customs rule the rearing of children.

American scientists recently discovered, with somewhat surprise, that new-born babies thrive best on their mother's milk. The secretion of a mother's milk is ruled by the prolactin hormone released by the pituitary gland, which activity is regulated by the hypothalamus, and the hypothalamus is easily influenced by the mind. A mother's mind, therefore, can control not only the quantity of milk, but also its quality. A mother's , milk, therefore, must provide not only nutrients, but also either the serenity or the anxiety in the mother's mind.

I feel that doctors who advise infertile women to carefully calculate the best time of the month, their ovulation period, etc..., to have sexual intercourse, must be wrong. The couple are then in a tense state of emotional arousal and in fear of failure, and under these conditions they usually fail to reproduce. If, instead, they were told to play with each other, and laugh and enjoy the act, far fewer people would be infertile.

HUMOUR AND SEXUAL DEVIATIONS

In most species it is the sex hormones that regulate mating patterns and behaviour. Stimulated through the senses and nervous system by external factors, usually light and temperature, the sex glands start releasing their hormones. This creates a sexual arousal, a biological discomfort, which is discharged by courting and mating.

In lower mammalians, mating is strictly conditioned by the female's readiness, by her seasonal fertility.

Due perhaps to their more developed playfulness, therefore more frequent bodily contact, monkeys and apes, however, often have sexual intercourse during the female's unproductive season.

As with other primates today, for millions of years human intercourse must have been mainly the result of the human female's sexual solicitation, or of playing, cuddling and hugging. With the development of the mind, however, humans became capable of creating sexual arousal with their fantasies. Playing with our imagination can trigger off the hypothalamo-pituitary-gonadal system, bringing sexual arousal. The erotic reveries of a man can produce erection and readiness for copulation. The sexual fantasizing of a woman increases her vaginal blood flow and the pulsations of her clitoris.

The mind's world also brought sexual deviations, unique to our speices, and typical of the adolescent mentality.

Perhaps one could understand certain psychosexual disorders better if one took into consideration that sexual arousal cannot take place during a strong psychosomatic arousal. The more inflated and the more obstinate an individual's mind, the less sexually aroused he becomes. Fervent religious or moral believers do not renounce sex: it is their beliefs that inhibit it. The rigidity of the mind's over-seriousness restrains the activity of the sex glands, therefore the excretion of their hormones.

It is in this inhibition of sexual arousal by a strong psychosomatic arousal, and in adolescent minded people's tendency to prove their virility and maturity through sexual activity, that we find the origins of many psychosexual deviations.

Some psychosexual deviations are, in fact, the discharge of a psychosomatic arousal in search of sexual excitement. This is best seen in voyeurism, exhibitionism, sodomy, bestiality and rape.

People with sexual deviations generally have one thing in common: an acute feeling of loneliness. They are desperate for intimacy, love and togetherness. They are victims of the adolescent mentality's style of life and culture in which sex is one of the most decisive factors in human interpersonal relationships.

As there is positive evidence that glandular or other physical conditions play only a slight part in the cause of psychosexual disorders, and as there is a stong indication that the mind plays an important role in these diseases, in my view, the best cure for these lonely people would be a sense of humour. By creating a relaxed atmosphere and a spirit of playfulness, a sense of humour helps to take over-seriousness less seriously. Taking the style of life and culture that give sex such a dominant role in interpersonal relationships humourously, could help those with sexual deviations.

Contracting or paralysing sexual organs, thus impeding the excretion of their hormones, a strong psychosomatic arousal can also cause impotence and frigidity. These can be of a temporary or lasting nature, depending on the duration and strength of the mind's created arousal. A strong psychosomatic arousal can also cause an anorgasmia in a female, her inability to reach an orgasm during intercourse, or vaginismus or vaginal spasms preceding the male's attempt to penetrate.

As people are capable of creating their own over-seriousness, the main cause of impotence and frigidity, in their imagination, why can they not use the same imagination to create playful and pleasant images in their minds which would reduce the psychosomatic arousal and result in relaxation and the body's elasticity, essential for sexual play? If the human mind can transform sex into a sin, then the same mind should be able to transform that sin into a joke, thereby liberating us from inhibition. The best lovers are those who do not take sexual activity over-seriously.

There are certain men who complain about premature ejaculation. This happens usually to those who consider sexual intercourse a performance. The fear of acting the role of lover inadequately, or the anxiety of not impressing his partner with his sexual prowess, usually causes this problem. In my view, the best cure for this could be simply to think of sexual intercourse as a play instead of a game, fun, rather than a test or a performance. In other words, instead of 'making' love, we should be playing at love or loving love.

One of the most known psychosexual disorders of the adolescent mentality's humanity is homosexuality.
In other mammalians, mainly under the pressure of high sexual arousal, both male and female individuals can display sexual behaviour which is characteristic of their opposite sex. This is probably due to the inheritance by the mammalians of a certain bisexuality. Humans are the only animals, however, who are able to show a definite preference for homosexuality.

What is the cause of this sexual deviation?
In his escape from reality into the fantasy world of his mind, an adolescent male usually forms his 'ought to be' ego around an ideal male figure. Some, however, are either unable to visualise such a figure, perhaps because their infancy was made miserable by their fathers, or they become disillusioned by their ideal male figure. These people frequently start idolising the opposite sex, their ideal woman.
An idealised female ego in the mind of a male encourages the

display of the feminine physical side he carries in him, and his homosexuality.

Lesbianism finds its origin in an excessive adoption or imitation by a woman of the male adolescent mentality. This usually occurs when in her infancy or early adolescence a girl has difficulty finding in her mother the ideal image she seeks, when she starts idealising masculine ego, when she starts encouraging the male side she carries in her. This attitude of mind ends in inhibiting the production and activity in her body of female hormones, and in stimulating those of male hormones, acquiring masculine behaviour and organising her sexual and emotional life in a masculine way.

Being an escape from failure or disillusion, the mind's world of a male homosexual is even more precarious and fragile than that of a heterosexual. This acute precariousness creates agitation and restlessness, which are frequently the main causes of his sexual insatiability and promiscuity.

A homosexual's inclination to dress in the fashion of the opposite sex, or his or her desire to change sex, comes naturally to a mind dominated by an idealisation of the opposite sex.

The above explanation can be applied to so-called active and aggressive female and male homosexuals. They pair and establish their sexual and amorous relationships usually with passive and submissive partners. One has the impression that these passive homosexuals' mental attitude stems from a halt in the transitory phase between infancy and adolescence. That is probably why they preserve a youthful look most of their lives, much longer than heterosexuals or active homosexuals of the same age. Perhaps this is due to their brains' mental activity under those particular emotional arousals produced by those special feelings of fragility and precariousness which were created by deprivation in the critical phases of their infancy of attention, protection or love, boys from their fathers, girls from their mothers.

Most passive homosexuals do not feel a real need for sex. In their immature minds, they fantasise about sex and its role. For them, sex becomes an instrument to reach intimacy and togetherness. Through physical contact and closeness, they try to reach the missed attention, protection or love.

As homosexuality is not a genetic or endocrine disorder but a creation of the mind, those unhappy with their state of existence could find their best solution in humour-therapy. In deriding idealisations, one reduces one's psychosomatic arousals, and this helps to reach a better mental and physical harmony.

A sense of humour could be a powerful help for AIDS, (Acquired Immuno-Deficiency Syndrome), this widespread disease among homosexuals. In my view, this disease is not so much caused by sexual practises between men, but by the particularly strong state of emergency and stress created by the male homosexual mind, by the permanent danger to which his idealised ego is exposed.

A sense of humour could also help to shake the present stereotypes of man and woman, created by the adolescent mentality and its culture.

CRIME, PUNISHMENT AND HUMOUR

In the field of juvenile crime and punishment, a serious problem in modern society, humour could play a significant role.

One of the main purposes of punishment, presumably, is to correct the criminal, to change him.

To a ruling order established by the adolescent mentality, a criminal is any individual with an excess of this mentality.

How can punishment correct criminals?

In knocking the criminals off their pedestals of excessive self-infatuation, self-righteousness or self-confidence, the adolescent mentality hoped to bring criminals back to infancy, infancy implying dependence and obedience. Punishment consisted and still consists of intimidation, torture and confinement.

Prisons or confinement camps, however, seldom work. Punishment is supposed to return criminals to infancy, but infants need to play. Play needs space and freedom of movement, which prisons and confinement camps do not provide.

There is a further reason why the present form of punishment is unsuccessful with habitual young criminals. These youngsters cannot be brought back to infancy with punishment, because on the whole, their infancy was their punishment in the first place. Statistics prove that most of today's habitual juvenile criminals have had a deprived childhood, and crave the play, joy, love and laughter that they missed out on in their childhood.

This is why humour, play and laughter should be the treatment used in re-education centres for habitual juvenile criminals. These youngsters cannot be shaken from their arrogance and self-centredness by punishment. If they were teased, however, and taught to laugh at themselves, they would see reality in a less selfish and dramatic way. What is more, humour also helps revive their mental alertness, which was so inhibited or confused by their unhappy childhood. There is evidence that about 40 percent of the habitual juvenile criminals in England are dim-witted.

Nowadays, re-education centres for young criminals try to inculcate a respect for the established order and authority. This cannot succeed because these centres are managed with rigidity and over-seriousness.

Those running these centres should bear in mind that the youngsters do not hate the actual establishment and its authority: what they hate is the idea of respect. Implying distance, the idea of respect nauseates them to the point of rage and insanity. It reminds them of selfishness, frigidity, repulsion and rejection, all of which they experienced in their infancy. What these young criminals really long for is understanding and playfulness, warmth and intimacy, togetherness and laughter.

Juvenile criminals would prefer to love the established order and authority, rather than respect it. In order to achieve this love, authority must relax its over-seriousness and rigidity, and start to develop a sense of humour.

Confronted with a humourous attitude, the youngsters might discover and develop their own sense of humour and self-ridicule. Authority should remember that juvenile criminals do not need a substitute for parents, they do not want a paternal or maternal Welfare State approach to their problems: what they are looking for is playmates.

Instead of fighting each other over-seriously, authority and habitual criminals should try and imitate the Greenland Eskimos who solve their quarrels by trying to outlaugh each other.

An unhappy infancy is not only found in broken homes, or in poor families with alcoholic or violent parents, but also in the most conformist or 'comme il faut' families where parents try to bring up their children in their own image, or where they try to impress their children by their own over-seriousness, success or brilliance.

Social services should organise special courses for couples

applying for marriage licences, the main subject being teasing. In fact, teasing should become a significant instrument in the education of children. Playful teasing helps to develop acuteness, a sense of humour and, above all, a sense of self-criticism in children. Any child is a potential juvenile delinquent. By teasing their children in their exaggerations or excesses, instead of dealing with them over-seriously, parents would prevent a good deal of juvenile crime. Parents should also be aware that whenever they treat their children over-seriously, it is not only for the childrens sake, but for their own. This selfishness is dearly paid for later by both children and their parents.

The following two accounts might give those dealing with the problems of teenage arrogance or habitual juvenile crime, an idea of my aim.

Returning one night late from a dinner party, an old-age pensioner noticed four youths leaning against a lampost, adopting a most aggressive attitude, in the street where he lived. Already under the influence of alcohol, he decided to appear much more so. Quickly loosening his tie and ruffling his hair, he started lurching and swaying like a total drunk, singing out of tune in an inarticulate manner. Approaching them he stumbled, grinned and with a loud hiccough, asked them to help him find the keyhole in his front door. Amused by the situation, the youths must have forgotten their aggressive intentions, and roaring with laughter, they helped the old man to enter his house.

My second example concerns the daughter of a friend of mine, recently graduated from both Oxford University and Teacher Training College. She took a job in the East End of London, teaching English to a class of menacing teenagers.

On her first day, as soon as she had opened her mouth, one of the boys shouted: 'Cor, Miss, you talk like the fucking Queen.'

When the general sniggering had subsided, she started again, a twinkle in her eye. 'I am so glad that one of you has mentioned the verb: to fuck. I will now begin my first lesson to you on the misuse of the English language.' Total silence reigned. 'The story I am going to tell you is an example of this. In the London Law Courts a sailor was suing his wife for adultery. The judge told him to explain simply, in his own way, what had occurred. "Well, your

Honour", the sailor began. "I disembarked from my fucking boat in Plymouth. I got the fucking train to fucking Victoria, then I took the fucking tube to my fucking house. I put my fucking key in the fucking lock, and what do I find? My wife having intercourse with the neighbour!"'

After this story, and by continuing to introduce togetherness and humour in her lessons, this girl soon became the most popular teacher in the school, and her class the most co-operative.

I am convinced that the first country to replace threatening and armed policemen with those armed with a sense of humour or a benign smile, would significantly reduce juvenile and all kinds of other crimes.

LEISURE

Ever since man began attributing so much importance to abstract speculations and philosophysing, he started considering work, particularly physical work, as degrading or humiliating.

The Ancient Greeks, who were proud of cultivating philosophy and abstractions, treated work as debasing or undignified. 'It is fitting for a man to despise work,' wrote Plato. 'All manual works are without nobility; it is impossible to cultivate virtue and to live as a wage-earner,' wrote Aristotle.

Many people today hold work in contempt. Bringing them to reality, work somehow mocks their conceit or illusions. Perhaps this is why incentives to work are so needed.

We have invented the idea of paradise, a typically adolescent paradise. In this paradise there is no effort or work, just free time for day-dreaming. J.J. Rousseau imagined the ideal primitive society as a society in which man had nothing to do. 'The produce of the earth furnished man with all he needed,' he wrote, 'so that singing and dancing, the true offspring of love and leisure, became the amusement, or rather the occupation of men and women assembled together with nothing else to do.'

Adolescents crave leisure. It pleases their conceited egos, but they often pay for it. Leisure increases an adolescent's sense of self-importance. This self-importance increases his pretentiousness, therefore his restlessness, and rushing. Rushing gives people the impression of contribution to their sense of self-importance. They never realise that in reality, rushing isolates them even more. It is a lonely activity which generates more loneliness. Rushing implies pushing and shoving which provokes the repulsion and revulsion of others.

The connection between leisure, restlessness and loneliness is evident with playboys, for example. They are usually young and healthy, often good-looking, with plenty of money and leisure time at their disposal. They are, however, often the loneliest and unhappiest people around.

Rushing has become so much a part of the life of Western man, that something is considered wrong with those who do not.

A Yugoslav painter I know emigrated to America. One day he was strolling in New York harbour, stopping from time to time to contemplate the boats and the landscape in view of painting a new picture. After a while he was stopped by the police as suspect.

In 1955 in Florence, I visited Giovanni Papini, one of the most serene writers of Italy. He was 74 years old. I asked him what he felt was the most negative change in his life-time. 'Rushing,' he answered. 'People used to work harder and longer, but still seemed to find time for others. They had time for a chat to friends. I remember a charming incident that happened to me about fifty years ago,' he told me. 'I was having a discussion with some friends in the middle of the Via Ghibellina late at night. A carozza rounded the corner, but on seeing us in deep conversation the driver changed direction in order to avoid disturbing us. Nowadays, in their selfish hurry, in their fast cars, people would run over a group of priests or even a pregnant woman, in order not to waste time.'

Western countries are proud of having so much leisure time. More and more people, however, are aware that this leisure time has also brought an increase in insomnia, anxiety, drug-addiction, suicide, and above all, an increase in psychosomatic diseases and mental disorders. The irony of our present way of living is that many scientists are beginning to discover that work-therapy is the best cure for the troubles caused by too much leisure.

Instead of helping to recuperate our lost energy, leisure time merely consumes our existing energy, and has succeeded in making people hate their work even more. This diminishes the productivity of work performance besides increasing accidents.

Many industrial accidents are caused by contempt for work.

In order to induce a little more enthusiasm and love for work I would suggest that the silly story of Adam's and Eve's punishment being hard work, sweat and toil following their rejection from Paradise, should be re-written as follows: 'Adam and Eve had been created by God and lived in paradise with all the comforts and leisure time in the world but they were miserable and bored, bored to death. "If we stay here a moment longer we will commit suicide," Eve complained to God. "We are so depressed. There is no fun in boredom, no love, no sex and no conception. Boredom makes people impotent. You said that you worked in order to create everything. Then let us out of paradise so that we, too, can create, that we too can work. It is selfish of you to keep us imprisoned here just to sit and worship you. With your computerised electronic eye you are the perfect gaoler. You see everything. You are omnipresent, permanently watching us, as if you were afraid of our escape. You are our nightmare."

'Hearing Eve's outburst, God had a heart attack. With the death of God, paradise vanished. Our Adams and Eves tilled the soil, grew their food, bred children and lived happily so long as the Eves were in charge.

'Humanity could have lived happily ever after if various Adams had not tried to replace the dead God with promises to rebuild the lost paradise. The humourous side of these promises is that in order to build a paradise one needs builders. But a God who promises paradise attracts those who hate work. Those who like work, however, laugh at the promises of gods, as they find paradise in their work.'

HUMOUR AS OUR ONLY SAVIOUR

If my theory about the nature of life is true, then a sense of humour is the only possible saviour of our species and of life in general.

I do not know what kind of electro-chemical processes took place some four billion years ago on our planet which created life out of matter, which transformed inorganic elements into organic compounds.

One thing, however, seems certain to me, which is that life was imposed on matter, that life was compelled on inorganic elements, and that life was forced on death.

Most probably, a mild sunlight energy and a temperate heat, with their weak fluctuations, and the moderate seasonal and circadian changes in some areas of our globe, were unable to transform some inorganic elements from one stable state into another. These mild and moderate operating forces brought certain inorganic elements into a vibrating precariousness, into a state of instability. Suspended in a state of uncertainty, these elements must have produced organic compounds with their irritations, agitation and fear.

Organic matter consists of inorganic elements in specific relation with the special external forces of our planet. There is no difference between the atoms of organic and inorganic matter. They are both dead matter.

If the sunlight energy and temperature, or their fluctuations had been more extreme, life on earth would never have appeared. If we succeeded in reducing the quantity of ozone in the atmosphere, or if the temperature of our planet changed radically, most of life would disappear.

Becoming organic, inorganic matter passed from a state of stability to a state of instability, from a state of comfort to a state of discomfort, from a state of quietude to a state of inquietude, fear and agitation. It is in the instability, discomfort, inquietude, fear and agitation of organic compounds that we find life. The fundamental laws of life are probabilistic which implies instability and fears. Life must have started with the tendency of organic matter to go from an unstable state back to the previous one of lasting stability, tranquility and comfort. Life consists, therefore, of activities aiming at eliminating fears and irritations which organic compounds carry in them. The main activities of life: eating, drinking and sex, are nothing but ways of eliminating or placating the fears caused by a biological irritation or discomfort. Instincts are instigated by chemical reactions.

Summed up, life could be defined as a chain of processes aiming at the everlasting state of order and stability, aiming at the original state of tranquility, aiming at death. Life, therefore, aims at the elimination of life, at the annihilation of itself.

Being the result of a special interaction between matter and energy, life cannot have an independent activity, it cannot reach its own stable state. It is not in life's power to eliminate itself, in spite of its tendency to do. In order to eliminate itself, life must be able to eliminate the forces creating it.

There is, however, one exception to this rule: adolescent humanity. They can find the energy to destroy life in their psychosomatic arousals. They can find the power and means to do this with their scientific and technological discoveries. They can find the desire to do this in the frustration and resentment caused by their failure to change nature to suit their inflated egos. We are the only species able to commit individual and collective suicide. Darwin was wrong when he wrote: 'That no species can in the long run behave contrary to the conditions of its survival.'

The natural tendency of life to reach a stable order and tranquility must have inspired the human mind's invention of dogmas, doctrines and moral principles. By leaning on them, humans must have hoped to achieve a certain solidity, tranquility, or order.

We are becoming more and more aware of the inability of our mind to find a system of ideas which offers this stability and tranquility. Religions have failed to provide a solid prop on which to lean. Socialism and Communism, these latest major creations of the human mind, have failed to realise their promised paradises.

More and more people are realising that the adolescent mind is unable to organise life in a rational way, or to bring peace and happiness. In 'War and Peace', Prince Andrei described the confused minds of Tolstoy and many others, when he said: 'There is nothing, nothing certain but nothingness of all that is comprehensive...'

The danger for life on our planet is increasing with this disillusion. What is more, this disillusion is expanding with the lengthening of our life-span, and the growing numbers of elderly people. With the lengthened life-span and old age, the mind's illusion, expectations and hopes are tested for longer, often ending in bitter disillusionment. The consequences of this is that people's selfishness becomes even blinder, and an infectious 'après moi le déluge' attitude is spreading.

In their growing pessimism and disillusionment, many, some consciously, others unconsciously, take pleasure in degrading or destroying life. In doing this, many also seem to feel that their conceit will then suffer less with their final departure. They consider that it is easier to leave an ugly life than a beautiful one.

It is only in this way that we can interpret human tolerance of the population explosion while natural resources rapidly dwindle. It is only in this way that we can understand our complacency towards the polution of our planet. It is only in this way that we can explain the increase in suicide, drug-addiction, alcoholism, greed, gluttony, and vandalism, along with the development of culture and civilisation. It is only in this way that we can understand the euphoria felt towards catastrophe and disaster. It is only in this way that we can explain the attraction for horror stories and films, the excitement for bad news. It is only in this way that we can understand our placid acceptance of the genetic degeneration of our species. It is only in this way that we can understand the growing destruction of the family, this nucleus of security. It is only in this way that we can explain the increasing need for rushing, and the exhilaration in adventure and audacity. It is only in this way that we can understand the thrill of gambling with nuclear weapons and energy, and the passion for destruction. ('The passion of destruction is a creative passion.' This thought of Bakunin reflects that of an increasing number of people.) It is only in this way that we can understand our indifference towards the progressive ugliness of life and the environment, and our unscrupulous exploitation and waste of natural resources. It is only in this way that we can understand the cynicism of so many scientists and their fever of excitement in trying to dominate nature. In his 'The Dialectics of Nature', F. Engels explained: 'Let us not flatter ourselves over much on account of our human conquest of nature. For each such conquest nature takes its revenge on us.' What Engels did not realise is that this was known to many, before and after him, but no-one has ever done anything to repair the error. The more we are aware of this truth, the more we provoke nature, as if we were desparately craving nature's revenge.

By considering life a joke of cosmic forces, a sense of humour could eliminate much of human destructiveness. Perhaps Wilhelm Raabe had this in mind when he said: 'We can only survive on the river of life if we float on a safety belt of humour.'

By taking life as a farcical play forced by sunlight energy on the inorganic matter which produced amino acids, these essential ingredients of proteins, by considering it a constant breakdown and repair, by knowing that each life's rhythmic beat or movement, like respiration, passes from near death to resuscitation, we can develop a certain tenderness for whatever is alive.

The meaninglessness of life is created by our mind's effort to give an ego-appealing meaning to life. Life is a gift of cosmic forces and a gift should provoke one, and only one reaction: that of gratitude.

COURSES IN A SENSE OF HUMOUR

Most schools today are run to suit the adolescent mentality. They prepare the young to be over-serious, self-confident, competitive and aggressive. They emphasise the value of the individual and his cult of self-importance which is at the expense of social and group life, therefore at the expense of the individual in the long run.

A sense of humour in schools could at least help in the problem of juvenile suicides. For the last twenty years, more and more teenagers have killed themselves. It is often their only way of solving the despair caused by their inability to cope with their first failures or emotional pressures. They cannot cope with these problems because they have been educated in an atmosphere of over-seriousness, an atmosphere in which problems are dramatised, in which failure is of catastrophic proportions. Only a sense of humour could de-dramatise these problems, can transform the rigidity of over-seriousness into the flexibility of seriousness, loneliness into togetherness and competition into cooperation. With a sense of humour one accepts failure with healthy sportiveness.

More than ever before, today's teenagers long for love. They should be taught that everyone loves those who laugh at themselves.

Some people are convinced that we are either born with a sense of humour, or not, that it is not something we can learn.

We are all born with a certain predisposition towards

playfulness, the joy of living, curiosity, exploration and flexibility, and we spend our infancy in that spirit.

With adolescence, however, we start learning, or imitating how to be over-serious or pretentious, how to pose or adapt best to an artificially created life.

If we can learn how to be over-serious, pretentious and to pose, surely we can learn how to be less over-serious, less pretentious and less affected. 'What lies in our power to do, it lies in our power not to do', as Aristotle said.

Learning a sense of humour, in fact, would mean the revival of our natural predisposition.

It is not easy, however, to advise people to reduce their self-importance, self-infatuation, beliefs, illusions or dreams, as these all act like drugs and tend to give us the impression of living a fuller and more purposeful life. Explaining that in the long run these drugs merely create misery, depression and unhappiness, is like telling an alcoholic that alcohol creates hangovers. The alcoholic knows this, but he likes it. A hangover gives him a reason to complain, which, in his immature way of thinking, contributes to his sense of self-importance.

It is even more difficult to convince people that the best cure for their problems, their disillusion, their psychosomatic troubles or mental disorders is a sense of humour or self-ridicule. Self-infatuated people become offended when advised to take themselves humourously. What is more, by taking ourselves too seriously, therefore seeing everything in hyperbolic or magnified proportions, we resent simple solutions to problems. Simplicity degrades us, toppling us from our pedestals of conceit.

I would like to try and contribute some advice which might help people to discover a sense of humour, and to be able to perceive life in more realistic dimensions. There is no problem, however dramatic or tragic it may seem, that has not got a humourous side, which, once perceived, dissolves the problem. 'There is no idea, no fact, which could not be vulgarised and presented in a ludicrous light', explained Dostoevski.

On the door of every classroom there should be a large sign inscribed in Chamfort's words: 'The most wasted day is that in which we have not laughed'.

Why should a day in which we have not laughed be wasted? Because laughter, both physically and mentally, is healthy. It rejuvenates us and brings us nearer to sanity, to common sense and reality. An Italian told me that he already knew by 1942 that Italy would lose the Second World War. He realised it when the Fascist Government prohibited laughter in public places. To him it was a sign of lost sanity. Nazi Germany did not even need to introduce legislation against laughter. No-one laughed in Nazi Germany, anyway. They were too exhausted coping with their wishful ideas of a super-race.

Through her popular writer, Martial, Ancient Rome gave the following advice: 'Ride, se sapis', meaning that the wise laugh.

As I have said, many people spend their whole lives afraid of being a laughing matter. This fear drives them to cheating, hypocricy, or meanness.

By developing a sense of self-ridicule, this fear would vanish. One way to achieve self-ridicule is to think of oneself in the third person, like one did as a child, or to talk to oneself in the mirror.

Courses in humour should emphasise that self-ridicule is not a sign of inferiority, but a sign of maturity.

In his 'The Tragic Sense of Life', Miguel de Unamuno wrote: 'The mortal Don Quixote, in dying, realised his own comicness and bewept his sins; but the immortal Quixote, realising his own comicness, superimposes himself upon it and triumphs over it without renouncing it... He (Don Quixote) will triumph by making himself ridiculous. And he will triumph by laughing at himself and making himself the object of his own laughter.'

These courses should advise people to see amusing and happy plays and films, and to read humourous books or magazines. The benefit of this can be deduced from the following passage in Fielding's 'Covent Garden Journal No. 10': 'Now whoever reads over the five great writers first mentioned in this paragraph must either have a very bad head, or a very bad heart, if he doth not become both a wiser and a better man'. The five writers that Fielding had mentioned were: Lucan, Cervantes, Swift, Shakespeare and Molière.

Our culture concentrates on praising success, but this merely magnifies the fear of failure. We take failure over-seriously, which drives us to excessive self-blame or self-contempt, resulting in unhealthy consequences.

By minimising failure, however, we reduce our fear of it. By reducing this fear we might acquire a certain serenity in which we have time to realise that most failures are basically funny, funny because our exaggerated expectations, based on our inflated self-appreciation, are deflated.

The best way to eliminate the tense state of competitiveness is by de-dramatising failure. This can be done by entering into the spirit of a good loser. If we did not mind losing, then, among other tiring emotions, we would eliminate envy, a major incentive to unscrupulous competition. If we did not mind losing we could eliminate from our system another unique emotion of our species: hatred. Hatred is the principal incentive for savage human aggression.

Much unhappiness is caused by the fallacy that successfully competitive people are happy. Those who envy successful competitors should remember that few of them achieve success in thier own eyes.

Many might argue that people with a sense of humour, understanding, gratitude or serenity could never be 'aggressive' or efficient enough from the point of view of economic productivity.

I would like to stress that a sense of humour, understanding, gratitude and serenity do not generate passivity and indolence, but exhuberance and radiance. What is more, with a more mature way of reasoning, created by a sense of humour, exhuberance and radiance are employed more intelligently, contributing therefore to social welfare and economic prosperity much more than neurotic and aggressive individual competition, inspired by an immature victor/victim or success/failure way of reasoning. Voluntary or charity work is evidence of this.

These courses should advise the opening of museums with permanent exhibitions of dolls, train sets and other toys, particularly in large industrial cities. One corner of everyone's home should be dedicated to toys, as their mere sight and feel lessens tension, thereby producing a good mood.

Staid protraits of ancestors, heroes or Saints tend to inspire over-seriousness and gloom. Instead, people should be encouraged to hang pictures of children and animals on the walls of their homes or offices.

Advertising, the modern opiate of the masses, should be taken more humourously. Advertising deforms reality and inhibits our natural taste and common sense values. What is more, advertising creates a mentality which is easily seduced by political propaganda.

These courses should teach that advertising and propaganda can disturb the joy of living and kill gratefulness. Advertising and propaganda create dissatisfaction, envy and resentfulness, all sources of tension and anxiety, aggression and destruction.

These courses should tell people of all ages to find a hobby. Hobbies eliminate tension and stress because they are a play on over-seriousness. It is advisable, however, to change the hobby the moment it is taken over-seriously.

Sailing or gardening, for example, would be beneficial, as these activities teach us that we cannot go against nature in the name of illusion or super-nature. Sailing and gardening only succeed if they are in harmony with the laws of nature.

People should be encouraged to have pets. More than 30 percent of the population of England lives alone. Playing with, talking to, stroking or cuddling a pet reduces the mind's activity, thereby reducing anxiety, stress and loneliess. Talking to pets and answering for them in a silly childish voice, helps playfulness and self-ridicule. Besides, there is scientific evidence that pets help to prevent, and in some cases cure, many psychosomatic diseases and mental disorders.

These courses should stress that we can only survive and find happiness in this life if we understand life. We can only understand life if we are in an understanding mood, or existence. The easiest way to reach this understanding mood would be with a sense of humour.

Knowledge can be a serious enemy to understanding. Knowledge brings pride, arrogance and blindness; that is why knowledge can bring sorrow, as is pointed out in the Bible. Instead of instilling as much knowledge as possible into children and teenagers, schools should teach them the best way to achieve understanding.

In understanding a problem we go further than solving it, we dissolve it. Understanding de-dramatises. Immature reasoning tries to solve a problem without understanding it, by imposing a wishful solution on it. This is why most of our problems are seldom solved.

These courses should emphasise that a great deal of technological and scientific progress is far beyond our needs. Most scientific explorations are not guided by the true necessities of humanity, but by scientists' search for importance, by their demiurgical aspirations. In Anthony Storr's 'The Dynamic of Creation' we read the following passage: 'Einstein's law of gravity was preferred to Newton's because it better explained certain discrepancies from Newton's hypothesis; notably an apparent anomaly in the motion of the perihelion of the planet Mercury.' Imagine how many people, the unemployed, and particularly those dying of starvation, were thrilled with this discovery. What a solace for those suffering from cancer the knowledge that we could see the world differently if we travelled at the speed of light.

Einstein clearly did not realise that if we travelled at the speed of light, we would be light, and light is seen but does not see.

The following story illustrates how many technological realisations are inspired by the search for prestige rather than for our needs. It is a conversation between two Russians.

Ivan: 'Have you heard that our enlightened Government has started producing supersonic aircraft?'
Alexis: 'How can that help me?'
Ivan: 'Well, if you hear on the media, for example, that a butcher in Leningrad is selling fresh meat, you can be in Novgorod in half an hour'.

Alexis: 'But why Novgorod? It is miles from Leningrad.'
Ivan: 'Because by the time you get there, the queue outside the shop in Leningrad will stretch as far as Novgorod.'

These courses should rewrite national histories. The national history of any country, from Albania to America, is always presented in the most glorified terms. This encourages arrogance, inflates pretentiousness, and creates national prejudices.

'What experience and history teach us is that people and government have never learnt anything from history or acted on the principles deduced from it', complained Hegel. But Hegel had obviously not realised that people and governments cannot learn from their own history for the simple reason that they invent and explain the past to suit the beliefs, prejudices or wishful thinking of the present.

Many amusing hours could be spent comparing the Russian, English, American, French, Italian and German national history, each about the same event.

One of the main duties of the United Nations should be to write national histories for its members in more objective terms. The European countries of the Common Market would have much more in common if they rewrote their national histories in less self-praising terms. By glorifying one's own country's past, one generally has to undermine the neighbouring countries. This does not make for togetherness.

The following lines written in a report by the coroner, after the assassination of Lord Mountbatten in Ireland, should be pasted all over the walls of offices of the United Nations: 'However, I believe it necessary to stress again the great responsibility that parents and teachers of any national have in the way they interpret history and pass it on to the youth of the country. I believe that if history could be taught in such a fashion that it would help to create harmony among people, rather than divison and hatred, it would serve this and all other nations better.'

The past of every country is filled with absurdities and incongruities, caprice, shortsightedness and misunderstanding, cowardice and failure, lies and treacheries, accidents and chance. Why, then hide them?

One of the absurdities of the last World War, and the period of post World War resettlement in Europe and the world, can be seen in the case of Great Britain. While the British people were heroically fighting for freedom, a major section of the British Intelligence Service was infiltrated by Communist spies, helping Communist domination throughout the world. The British would be in better shape had their leaders in charge of Intelligence read the following passage from Carlyle's 'Sartor Resartus': 'The man who cannot laugh is not only fit for treason, stratagems and spoils, but his whole life is already a treason and a stratagem'.

Victor Hugo was right when he claimed that the result of the Battle of Waterloo was due to chance, that it might have had a different outcome had it not rained the night before. Anglo-French relations would have been better had their national histories emphasised the role of chance in human events.

If national histories were taught more humourously, then history would serve its purpose and even indicate some of its logic, therefore become less of a contingency. In his book 'De l'humour', Georges Elgozy stressed: 'If history does not teach us anything useful it is because it is expurgated of humour'.

These courses in a sense of humour could explain that with a less dramatised and less glorified past, the present would be happier and the future more hopeful.

One can de-dramatise many situations that arise in life by seeing them thorough an analogous joke or a humourous anecdote. These courses should therefore advise memorising as many of them as possible.

For example, one could put up with fanatic do-gooders, particularly politicians, by remembering the following story:

A scout master advised his pack of cubs to do a good deed every day, such as helping an old person across a busy street. The following day he asked them what they had done, most surprised to learn that all twelve of them had helped one old lady to cross the road.

'Was it necessary for all of you to help?' He enquired.

'Oh yes,' replied the pack leader. 'You see, the old woman didn't want to cross the road.'

We could face the arrogance of modern painting and those who consider us inferior if we criticise it, by reminding ourselves of this anecdote.

Picasso employed an Italian gardener. One day he decided to ask the old man's opinion of his work. In Picasso's studio the following dialogue took place:
Gardener: 'What is this?'
Picasso: 'It's a woman.'
Gardener: 'A woman?'
Picasso: 'That is how I see a woman.'
Gardener: 'And that one?'
Picasso: 'A horse.'
Gardener: 'A horse?'
Picasso: 'That is how I see a horse.'
Gardener: 'Signor Picasso, with such terrible eyesight, what made you decide to try and paint?'

The following story could help us when faced by unaesthetic behaviour:

A youth sitting opposite an English lady in a train was chewing gum in a most unattractive manner. 'Young man,' the lady smiled, 'it is very kind of you to make, what I'm sure is fascinating conversation, but sadly I am deaf, so please don't bother.'

The following descriptions of a High Mass, as seen through the eyes of a child on his first visit to church, might help people to take religious ceremonies less over-seriously:

'There were a lot of people but they all looked cross or sad. Obviously the owners of the Church were poor, as there was no lighting or heating, just candles. Most people were whispering and some were counting the beads on their necklaces to check that none were missing. A lot of people were sleeping as they had their eyes shut. Suddenly there was silence and everyone stood up. A man wearing a lady's gold and red dress, with a tall gold hat walked slowly up to the table at the top, followed by other men and boys wearing frilly white shirts. The gold and red man went behind the table and came back again without his hat. I suppose someone had stolen it, because he started wailing very loudly and waving his arms around. Then the other men and boys all joined in to look for it, but all they found was a big heavy book. He must have got quite dirty looking for it, so they brought some water and a towel so that he could wash his hands. After a while they decided that he must have a new hat, so someone passed plate round and everyone put money onto it. They must have collected quite a lot, as there was enough for most people to go up to the table and get a free drink and a biscuit. Then suddenly the man went behind the table and came back with his hat on. He smiled and opened his arms to everyone, obviously very pleased to have found it, but he forgot to give the money back.'

Bearing in mind the following fable might help us to laugh at the increasing pessimism which surrounds today's world:

'Once upon a time there were two frogs. One was an optimist, of a cheerful and happy nature, able to see the funny side of everything. The other was a pessimist, gloomy and over-serious. One day they both fell into a large milk churn. "How awful. We'll never get out of here and we cannot survive in milk," the pessimistic frog sighed. "We are going to die, and die in agony. I don't want to suffer. I would rather kill myself." He banged his head hard against the side of the milk churn and sank like a stone.

"Well, I'm not going to commit suicide," the optimistic frog said. "If I've got to die, I'm going to die happy. I shall have one last fling."

'With these words the optimist began splashing round and round, dancing and singing. After a while, he noticed that his exhuberant movements were turning the milk to butter. Soon he was able to climb out, and leap to safety.'

The simplest and most effective lesson on how to face a new day with more of a sense of humour is to repeat every morning three times: 'I am not the centre of the universe.' With this in mind, one could see anyone who thinks they are the centre of universe, as pathetic, thus liberating us from fears of these kind of people.

There is one sentence that everyone should use as the best instrument for de-dramatising arrogant and argumentative

people: 'I'm sorry, I thought you had a sense of humour.'
It has a magic effect. Everyone tries to prove one wrong.

It is this aspiration to have a sense of humour that gave me confidence that a sense of humour can be our saviour.

PART II

In the second part of this book I would like to try and expose the ridiculous side of certain beliefs, preconceptions or achievements of the adolescent mentality, hoping that this might help to reach a maturer reasoning.

Something must be wrong with the present way of thinking, if, throughout most of the world, half of both human and natural resources are spent on the police, military and nuclear powers to keep these beliefs, preconceptions and achievements valid and operating. Perhaps it is this increasing police, military and nuclear protections of these beliefs, preconceptions and achievements that makes the world such a gloomy place to live in.

SELF-IMPORTANCE

One of the damaging inventions of the human mind in its adolescent phase of thinking is self-importance. But, in this phase we need self-importance. We need it in order to impress ourselves, and we need to impress and encourage ourselves because of our fear of self-ridicule due to our pretentiousness. According to Webster's Dictionary, self-importance is 'an exaggerated estimate of one's importance or merit'...'a self-conceit'.

Individual self-adulation and self-importance started expanding in Europe with Greek philosophy. In the VI Century B.C. Pythagoras, in his 'Golden Maxims', gave the following advice to man: 'Respect yourself most of all.' A century later Protagoras stressed that 'Man is the measure of all things.' Aristotle pushed Greek arrogant self-infatuation even further when he said: 'Nature was right because it has produced a species, slaves, who use their bodies to replace our fatigue'...'It is right and reasonable that Greeks should rule over Barbarians for the latter are slaves by nature, and the former are free men.'

Man's favourite motto is 'know thyself'. Most people are aware of this flattering piece of advice of Socrates, because it appeals to their self-centredness. Few people remember that Menander, a leading writer of the Greek 'New Comedy' said something far more revealing but less appealing: 'The saying "know thyself" is silly. It would be more practical to say: "know other folk".'

Few recall A. Gide's important truth as it also lacks appeal to the self-importance mania. "Know thyself" is a maxim as pernicious as it is ugly', he said. 'Whoever observes himself arrests his own development. A caterpillar who wanted to know itself well could never turn into a butterfly.' Perhaps this is why the human species has not yet reached maturity.

Self-importance is a major source of aggression, its definition being 'an exaggerated estimate of one's own importance and merit.' The aim of any 'exaggerated estimate' is to realise itself, which can only be done through aggression at someone else's expense.

Self-importance generates the human passion for dramatisation. In our longing to become 'dramatis personae' we create dramas and tragedies. Tragedies have a 'certain magnitude' as Aristotle said.

In order to remain in power, politicians often create major international dramas just to increase people's sense of self-importance, making them insensitive to local or personal problems. Self-importance exposes us to easy seduction.

In order to make life appeal more to our self-importance, we often create unnecessary complications. As the German humourist wrote: 'Why do things simply when you can complicate them.'

Many people just complicate their lives so as to be able to complain, as complaining gives us an illusion of importance. 'Why, since we are always complaining of our ills, are we constantly employed in redoubling them?' asked Voltaire in his 'Candide'.

Self-importance is a great enemy of both communication and relationships. This is unfortunate as self-importance craves communication and relationship, but cannot achieve them because the craving is in order to be recognised and applauded.

Self-importance also breeds boredom.

When, in his 'Don Juan', Byron wrote that: 'Society is formed of two mighty tribes, the bores and the bored,' he was inaccurate. The bores and the bored are one and the same tribe. Concentrated only on themselves, therefore insenstive, the bored are bores.

We consider ourselves superior to nature. 'Maîtres actuel de la planète tèrre', as Cousteau stressed before starting his campaign against the pollution of the seas.

There is one thing that has always puzzled me. If humans feel so superior, why are they not livelier and happier? Why do they spend their whole lives trying to escape from the reality of nature into illusions and fantasy?

In proportion to body-size, we possess the biggest brain in the animal world. We are proud of this, but a brain that can invent the idea of pride cannot be right. How ironic to be so proud of our big brain. One simple fantasy, one small prejudice, is capable of blocking its entire rationality. One trivial belief can manipulate our brain to the point of blindness.

Self-importance generates the idea of importance. Humans create and cultivate importance in order to be able to integrate into it, therefore increasing their own personal importance.

We glorify humanity merely to boost our self-importance, always identifying ourselves with the object of our admiration.

There are many books illustrating the achievements of our species, but few that mention its failures.

We glorify our national past and we identify ourselves with it to flatter our sense of self-importance. We create celebrities in order to feel important applauding them, following them and meeting them. The applause, however, is usually self-applause.

We build important places in order to gain more self-importance by visiting them.

Many people go to the theatre merely to witness a hit, thereby feeling part of it. Many people attend the opera or ballet just to be seen, to feel important.

Obsession with self-importance encourages the adolescent mentality's excesses and exaggerations, these enemies of natural order, harmony and above all of taste. Excess kills excellence.

In his 'Meditations', Marcus Aurelius stressed: 'Remember this, – that very little is needed to make a happy life.' This wise advice sadly only appeals to a minority. The majority of humanity are not looking for a happy life, but an important one.

SELF-REALISATION

I would now like to expose the ridiculous side of self-realisation, yet another obsession of humanity.

Self-realisation, self-fulfillment, self-assertion and self-actualisation are considered sacred rights. Self-realisation is an established ethical doctrine which explains that human individuals should be free to fulfill or assert themselves.

Man, however, never asks himself if his 'self' is mature, right or justified enough to become a reality. Crime, after all, is nothing but self-realisation.

I would like to repeat that the human self is nothing but an artificially created idea, an abstract and wishful speculation. Self-realisation, therefore, can only have one meaning: forcing reality to suit an idealisation. One's self can only be asserted, therefore, through aggression, violence, force, blackmail, treachery or bribery.

Psychiatry explains that if 'wretched man' is not self-fulfilled, he may become frustrated, irritated or depressed. Psychiatry never took into consideration one important fact: if the 'wretched man' achieved his self-fulfillment, his family, his neighbours and his society might suffer from frustration, irritation or depression.

Psychiatry seldom asks if man's unhappiness, frustration and depression are not caused by exaggerated self-esteem and selfish over-ambition. Psychiatrists should deride this selfish over-ambition. They should explain that any victory in the self-fulfillment of the over-ambitious creates even more frustration and unhappiness, as with his self-fulfillment he will find himself in an even more precarious position. They should also explain that any self-fulfillment of the over-ambitious can only be realised at the expense of his community, and this turns him out of the community into loneliness.

One might see the ridiculous side of the idea of self-assertion and its right to existence and freedom, if for a moment one imagined a society in which everyone, everyone from the extreme left to those on the extreme right, succeeded in realising his ideal self.

RELIGION

Any religion, if not taken over-seriously, is basically humourous. A believer in one relgion realises this when hearing of the revelations of others. 'Every religion but their own is an invention of men, while their own religion is an emanation from God,' said Marx.

Marx reproached religion for being 'the opiate of the masses.' He was obviously unaware that the adolescent mentality loves being drugged by illusions and beliefs.

That is probably why he was successful with his own illusions and beliefs. Only those capable of believing in super-nature, afterlife or resurrection can believe in the ideations or Utopiae of Marx and others like him. Believing in a God, to put it simply, means that our mind is open for seduction to any other belief, any absurd illusion or any ludicrous political or economic idology.

In fact, most religions must have a poor opinion of human intelligence. They treat their believers like half-witted infants who need strict commandments.

Religion reaches a humourous state when it preaches that believers should love their God. 'True religion must have as a characteristic, the obligation to love God,' explained Pascal. In His omniscience, surely God should know that love has to be deserved. He should also know how dangerous those who love Him can be. Some of the most atrocious crimes in history have been committed by lovers of God.

God must be pretty desperate if He needs the love of a species

He considers sinful, a species which invented Auschwitz, the Gulag and Apartheid.

Religion also inhibits human communications. A fervent believer communicates primarily with his God, thus alienating himself from his fellow men.

The Christian Church has noticeably contributed to hypocrisy.

Imagine what would happen if Christ suddenly appeared on the steps of St. Peter's in Rome, or Westminster Abbey in London, today, for example, and with outstretched arms, announced that he had returned to Earth to explain God's revelations on the matter of material wealth. There is no question that he would be locked in a mental home for impersonating Jesus Christ. A similar treatment would be accorded to Marx if he re-appeared in the Kremlin. His future would be a psychiatric hospital or a re-education centre in Siberia.

So-called Original Sin, the penalty we pay for 'Adam's fall' is another idea which could be taken with a pinch of salt.

The purpose of punishment is to correct a sinner or a criminal, and to prevent further sin and crime. Punishment cannot correct a sinner who has inherited a sin, and even less prevent a sin which, according to God, we are born with.

There is positive evidence that the first human beings evolved from other primates. The beginning of the human species was caused by some mutation in our ancestors' genes. Surely we cannot be punished for biological mutations. God has not punished amphibians because they evolved from fish, or mammals because they evolved from amphibians, or primates because they evolved from mammals. Why therefore, should He punish man because he evolved from primates?

In Milton's 'Paradise Lost' we read God's view about Adam's fall: 'I made him just and right, sufficient to have stood, though free to fall.' The human species were not 'free to fall'. Natural mutations are not ruled by free will.

In order to take 'original sin' more humourously, one should ponder about the following amusing absurdity. If everyone took the dogma of Original Sin with the religious fervour of strong believers, the human species would die out. Fervent believers should cease procreation to prevent the greatest sin of all: the procreation of sinners.

'THE SAD REALITY'

We enjoy complaining that life is tough, that reality is 'sad' because it is filled with violence, hatred, intolerance, envy and jealousy.

We consider ourselves fortunate, however, as we are able to escape this 'sad reality' by hiding in a world of illusions, fantasies and day-dreams, but we seldom realise that it is, in fact, the world of illusions, fantasies and day-dreams that is sad.

Reality is not sad: it is full of life. The world of illusions is a world of disappointments and disillusions, therefore a world of ugliness, cruelty, violence, hatred, bitterness, intolerance, envy and jealousy.

In the world of illusions, everyone longs for his day-dreams to come true. This is what creates a 'sad reality', a 'pathetic world'. Day-dreams can only be realised at the expense of others' day-dreams. Everyone tries to realise his day-dreams by unscrupulously exploiting the day-dreams of others. Unscrupulousness is in the nature of day-dreaming, and this is what makes our world of illusions and day-dreams a 'sad reality'. When our day-dreams are shattered, we consider it unfair, but day-dreaming itself is unfair, unfair to the day-dreams of others, unfair to reality, unfair to life. To avoid this, perhaps we had better start deriding our own day-dreams and self-deception. We can, because, as Goethe, said: 'We are never deceived; we deceive ourselves.'

By escaping the 'sad reality', we are escaping from one illusion or day-dream, in which we were exploited and disillusioned, into another.

The present world is a world of the continuous conversion from one illusion or day-dream to another. When a believer is disillusioned in his belief, mainly because he discovered that he was exploited, instead of deriding himself, he opts for another belief with renewed fervour.

The most negative side of illusions and day-dreams is their inclination to prevent us from maturing. We are too fascinated by our game of the exploitation of the mind's creativity.

We seldom realise, however, that illusions and day-dreams isolate us, increasing our sense of precariousness and loneliness, therefore our anxiety and despair.

Hiding behind their illusions and day-dreams, people do not understand that they impoverish themselves, depriving themselves of the wealth of life and its variety. 'Life is infinitely richer than whatever your imagination may invent,' said Dostoevski.

EASTERN ESCAPISM

Unhappy with their 'sad reality', many people search for a solution to their problems in the Eastern attitude.

In his conceit, Western man tries to change nature and reality to suit his self-created image of himself. Eastern philosophic and religious tradition, however, insists that, being divine, man should have no consideration for the realm of reality, but just ignore it. The supreme aim of eastern philosophy is the recovery of this 'divine self'.

In his book, 'The Eye of Shiva', A. de Riencourt explains that 'in the East, man is potentially divine and all he has to do is to strip away the veils of ignorance created by the phenomenal material world and mental acitivity that goes with it; he must dispel the unreal world of "maya" in order to reach identification with his true, timeless "Self".'

In the 'Tibetan Book of the Great Liberation', it is written that 'just as a pearl-hunter, aided by heavy stones tied to his feet, dives to the bottom of the ocean and secures the precious pearl, so should man, aided by indomitable will, dive deep within himself and secure the most precious of jewels: the Self.'

Another piece of text from 'The Eye of Shiva' proves that Eastern man tries to 'recover' the Self which has already been created by his self-adulation, and then to 'identify' his glorious self-made image with the idea of god, which his mind has created to suit his Self.

'The fundamental problem of Eastern consciousness is to bring about the identification of the Self with the Ultimate Subject, that is, the identification of the Self with Brahman, the Godhead. Tantric meditational techniques, for example, direct the seeker to visualise, at first, a divine image and then to "identify" with it; this is based on the premise that "one cannot venerate a god unless one is a god oneself", implying the actual awakening and recovery of one's own inner divinity.'

Eastern man's 'recovery of Self' is not so candid and naive as many think, but a calculated volition of his mind. If Eastern man could succeed in eliminating his mind's world, its fantasies and its abstractions, as he pretends he can, he would become joyful, playful and full of a sense of humour.

By falling into a state of drowsiness, insensitivity and intertia, a cataleptic state, Eastern man finds his Self, his most 'precious of all jewels'.

In fact, an Oriental mystic resembles a self-made freak of nature rather than a wise man.

What is this external world from which Eastern man is so proud to escape?

Basically it is his old mother, his invalid father, his defenceless children, his neighbours, his society, his species, his responsibilities: in other words, he is escaping from life itself, and above all, from work.

Buddha abandoned his family, which, according to him, became 'unreal' and 'an illusory realm'.

The Eastern mystic's attitude creates a sad situation, in which every man is alone, in which there is no togetherness, 'joie de vivre' or laughter. 'Every man is grave alone', as Emerson stressed. The joke is that these pathetic individuals, isolated in their conceit and far removed from reality, consider themselves to be 'spiritually enlightened'.

I believe that humour and laughter can bring more enlightenment than any Eastern escapism. Humour and laughter bring exuberance, a healthy interest in life, and a love of work, which Eastern mystics detest since they think it is degrading. It is curious, however, to note that while Eastern men proudly meditate, their women work.

The following quote from Gita Mehta's book, 'Karma Cola', an expert on both Eastern and Western culture, illustrates what I am trying to point out.

' " I left the ashram because it's so corrupt. The guru never stops playing favourites."... ."It's rather sick really. The people who are rich get closer to the guru than those who are poor."..."In the end I stopped caring about guru contact. I just got tired o having to do all the dirty jobs, while the rich powerful guys sat around being holy."...

'No-one heeded Ravi Shankar when he pleaded with his audiences: "Get high on the music, it is enough."

'Nothing was enought to those who had heard the sirens scream Turn on, Tune in, Expand your Mind.

'Alas, the mind can be expanded until it bursts, and when it does there stands an Indian parental type saying, Oh yes, this is a common mind-expansion problem, bursting. It has been going on in our country for about four thousand years. Why not come to my ashram? I will heal your mind if you give me your soul'...

'The metaphysical tourist wants that smile on the Buddha's face, the serenity of the cosmic orgasm. To him the novelty specialty guru says, If you're good, I'll make you feel good.'

ESCAPE INTO THE PAST

Unhappy with their 'sad' present, many people dream about what they imagine as a glorious period in the past, mainly the romatic era of the last century.

In order to help these people to discover the beauty of the present, I would like to advise them to read certain comments the great representatives of the romatic era expressed about each other.

One of the greatest romantics, Lord Byron referred to the consumptive John Keats as the following: 'Here are Johnny Keats' piss-a-bed poetry, and three novels by God knows whom...no more Keats, I entreat: flay him alive, if some of you don't I must skin him myself: there is no bearing the drivelling idiotism of the Mankin.'

In 1818, this is what Blackwood's popular 'Quarterly Review' wrote on Keats' work: 'The Phrenzy of the "Poems" was bad enough in its way; but it did not alarm us half so seriously as the calm, settled, imperturbably drivelling idiocy of "Endymion"... Mr. Hunt is a small poet, but he is a clever man. Mr. Keats is a still smaller poet, and he is only a boy of pretty abilities, which he has done everything in his power to spoil... We venture to make one small prophecy, that his bookseller will not a second time venture £50 upon anything he can write. It is better and wiser to be starved as an apothecary than as a poet; so back to the shop, Mr. John back to 'plasters, pills and ointment boxes.'...

'Commenting on Monckton Milnes' 'Life of Keats', Thomas

Carlyle stressed: 'Fricassee of dead dog... A truly unwise little book. The kind of man that Keats was gets ever more horrible to me. Force of hunger for pleasure of every kind, and want of all other force, such a soul, it would once have been very evident, was a chosen "vessel of Hell".'

Keats was not so sentimental towards his contemporaries, either. 'Wordsworth,' he said, 'has left a bad impression wherever he visited in town by his egotism, vanity and bigotry.'

This is how unromantically the 'Quarterly Review' viewed Shelley. 'Mr. Shelley is a very vain man; and like most vain men, he is but half instructed in knowledge and less than half disciplined in reasoning powers: his vanity ... has been his ruin.'

'Shelley,' Carlyle explained, 'is a poor creature who has said or done nothing worth a serious man being at the trouble of remembering.. Poor soul, he has always seemed to me an extremely weak creature; a poor, thin, spasmodic, hectic shrill snd pallid being ... The very voice of him, shrill, shrieky, to my ear has too much of the ghost.'

To Robert Southey, Shelley was a liar and a cheat; 'He paid no regard to truth, nor to any kind of moral obligation.'

Algernon Swinburne described Lord Byron as 'the most affected of sensualists and the most pretentious of profiligates.'

John Styles considered Byron as 'a denaturalised being who, having exhausted every species of sensual gratification, and drained the cup of sin to its bitterest dregs, is resolved to show that he is no longer human, even in his frailties, but a cool, unconcerned fiend.'

The following is what Lord Byron thought of some of his contemporaries: 'I have no patience with the sort of trash you send me out by way of books ... I never saw such work or works. Campbell is lecturing, Moore idling, South twaddling, Wordsworth drivelling, Coleridge muddling, Joanna Baillie piddling, Bowles quibbling, squabbling and snivelling.' 'Let simple Wordsworth chime his childish verse, And brother Coleridge lull the babe at nurse.'

Thomas Carlyle reviewed William Wordsworth in the following way: 'For prolixity, thinness, endless dilution, it excels all the other speech I had heard from mortals ... The languid way in which he gives you a handful of numb unresponsive fingers is very significant.'

In the 'Quarterly Review' one can read these lines on William Hazlitt: 'He abuses all poets, with the single exception of Milton, he abuses all country-people, he abuses the English; he abuses the Irish; he abuses the Scotch ... if the creature ... must make his way over tombs of illustrious men, disfiguring the records of their greatness with the slime and filth which marks his track, it is right to point him out, that he may be flung back to the situation in which nature designed that he should grovel'... 'A mere ulcer, a sore from head to foot, a poor devil so completely flayed that there is not a square inch of healthy flesh on his carcass; an overgrown pimple, sore to the touch.'

To Coleridge, Hazlitt's manners were '99 in a 100 singularly repulsive.'

To Carlyle, Coleridge was 'A weak, diffusive, weltering, ineffectual man ... Never did I see such apparatus got ready for thinking, and so little thought. He mounts scaffolding, pulleys and tackle, gathers all the tools in the neighbourhood with labour, with noise, demonstration, precept, abuse and sets, three bricks.'

On Carlyle, Samuel Butler wrote: 'It was very good of God to let Carlyle and Mrs. Carlyle marry one another and so make only two people miserable instead of four.'

The following is what John Ruskin had to say about Whistler's painting. 'I never saw anything so impudent on the walls of any exhibition, in any country, as last year in London. It was a daub professing to be a "harmony in pink and white" (or some such nonsense); absolute rubbish, and which had taken about a quarter of an hour to scrawl or daub, it had no pretence to be called painting. The price asked for it was two hundred and fifty guineas'... 'I have seen and heard much of cockney impudence before now; but never expected to hear a coxcomb ask two hundred guineas for flinging a pot of paint in the public's face.'

Here is what Max Nordau said on John Ruskin: 'Ruskin is one of the most turbid and fallacious minds ... of the century. To the service of the most wildly eccentric thoughts he brings the acerbity of a bigot ... His mental temperament is that of the first Spanish Grand Inquisitor. He is a Torquemada of aesthetics .. He would burn alive the critic who disagrees with him ...Since stakes do not stand within his reach, he can at least rave and rage in word, and annihilate the heretic figuratively by abuse and cursing.'

I hope that these quotes might awaken people's day-dreams of their glorified view of the 'romantic' past. 'The unhappiest man', according to Kierkegaard, 'is someone who lives in past memory or future hope, someone incapable of savouring the present and obsessed instead with inventing ways to make the time pass by.'

REVOLUTIONS

Some people try to avoid their present by escaping into the world of political ideologies, by dedicating themselves to a revolutionary cause. To a revolutionary, political ideology is merely a useful means to discharge his massive psychosomatic arousal, created by his particularly strong self-opinionated self. A revolutionary does not serve his chosen ideology, he uses it to destroy the existing order, his present. A revolutionary knows that a new order, in the name of which he is destroying the existing one, will not help him to alleviate his discontent as the new present will be even less appealing to his excessive self-conceit. In fact, many revolutionaries continue to rebel even after their revolution has succeeded. Stalin was a great political psychologue. In order to save Communism in Russia, he eliminated most of the revolutionaries. He knew that revolutionariness was a chronic mental disorder, caused by excessive self-opnionativeness, aiming at destroying any existing order. In fact, Western Communists never want to live in Communist countries, as they know only too well that there they would be in trouble, as there they would be dissidents.

The following facts may illustrate the paradox of revolutions.

Revolutions destroy a previous way of life in order to build a 'new' one. But the revolutionaries have to then build this new life on what is left. The remains of a revolution are the same human element, the same natural resources, the same traditions, the same language, the same climate, the same lands, the same factories, the same workers and the same politicians. All politicians, whether

155

left wing or right, have the same mentality.

In order to succeed, a revolution has to adapt itself to the existing conditions, conditions of life that it destroyed. Revolutions in nature caused by mutations, after all, are eliminated if they cannot adapt to the existing environment.

Revolutions are rather similar to children playing with bricks or building card-houses. After a time, they knock them down, then start to build new ones. The new ones only give the impression of being new because the various cards or bricks are broken or torn, victims of destructions.

A revolution simply turns evolution back to a previous point of departure. The actual word revolution derives from the Latin word 'revolvere', meaning to roll back, to return to the starting point in order to revolve again. The following story might illustrate revolutions' futility.

When Stalin died he met up with the last Tsar.

Tsar: 'Tell me, how is life in our great country now. Is the almighty father of all Russians still in the Kremlin?'

Stalin: 'Yes'.

Tsar: 'Is there still only one belief dictated by the Kremlin?'

Stalin: 'Yes'.

Tsar:: 'Is there still our powerful secret police enforcing the belief dictated by the Kremlin?'

Stalin: 'The same'.

Tsar: 'What about our privileged aristrocracy?'

Stalin: 'We call it nomenclatura.'

Tsar: 'And what happened to the bourgeoisie?'

Stalin: 'We replaced it with bureaucracy.'

Tsar: 'And our corrupt administration?'

Stalin: 'The same'.

Tsar: 'And our lazy peasants?'

Stalin: 'Still the same'.

Tsar: 'Do you still send mad people like writers and intellectuals who dare to criticise official beliefs to Siberia or into exile?'

Stalin: 'Of course'.

Tsar: 'And do you still produce our wonderful vodka at 63 percent proof?'

Stalin: 'Oh, no. We now have vodka at 65 percent proof.'

Tsar: 'Was the revolution really worth while just for two extra degrees of vodka?'

Someone rightly said that a revolution is nothing else but shifting the boot of tyranny to another foot.

Every successful revolution has to replace the monuments to previous martyrs with its own. Martyrs of all eras are the same. Unable to live, they die for a cause. In living for it they would damage the cause. John Burgoyne understood this when, in 'The Devil's Disciple' he wrote: 'Martyrdom ... is the only way in which a man can become famous without ability.'

SCIENCE AND TECHNOLOGY

I would now like to discuss a few aspects of science and technology which might help the reader to view them with less veneration.

Over the past two centuries, we have been fascinated by the progress of science and technology. The danger of a fascination, however, is that it obscures common sense, thus preventing any advancement towards a clearer way of reasoning.

By nature we are more exploratory than any other species, and science is a result of this characteristic. But beyond a certain level, scientific exploration can damage the relationship between man and nature. Both become losers. We have now reached the point in which we destroy and kill in order to explore, and this is becoming a perverse game for more and more people.

It is interesting to note that any improvement or discovery in science and technology increases a tension in the atmosphere, and an arrogance in the group, country or political belief of the discoverer.

Between the two World Wars, Germany produced more scientific discoveries and technological realisations than most other countries. At the same time, the Germans committed more atrocities than anyone else. The further that Communist Russia advances in science and technology, the more oppressive the regime becomes, and the more powerful and feared the police. Russians can travel into space, but not to Paris.

What is even more dangerous is that any new scientific or technological discovery in arms, increases our aggressiveness and destructiveness. It is in the nature of a discoverer to want to experiment with his discoveries.

At the beginning of the scientific age, many people thought that science would increase the sense of reality. The XIX Century, the century of science and technology, however, was also the century of a revival of religions and political utopias, and the damage caused by these was far greater than the advantages brought by science and technology.

We are finally beginning to realise that technological progress does not make for happiness. We have even reached a stage in which some people do not know the meaning of happiness.

On April 29th, 1980, London's 'Evening Standard' brought out the following articles, both on the same page: 'Life's good in Britain' and 'The booze woos young drinkers'. The first article read: 'Britain has never had it so good, says the General Household Survey of 1978. More of us now have fridges, central-heating and colour televisions than at the beginning of the decade, and the vast majority of us are happy with our homes.' Two paragraphs away was written: 'According to the General Household Survey for 1978, 40 percent of young men aged between eighteen and twenty-four drink heavily.'

Humanity was fascinated by science, mainly because it was convinced that science would provide or inspire a more stable morality, a more rational ethic. Humanity has been disillusioned.

What are the ultimate achievements of this science which promised so much?

The main achievements of science are the following: Einstein's 'Theory of Relativity', Heisenberg's 'Principle of Uncertainty', Nuclear Physics' 'Unpredictability', Jacques Monod's 'Le Hasard' and Planck's Quantum Theory's 'Probability Amplitude'.

In a Universe ruled by relativity, uncertainty, chance, unpredictability or probability amplitude, there is no way of creating a stable morality or a scientific ethic. What's more, modern physics can only speculate about the 'mysterious background' out of which matter springs. We seem to be learning more and more about less and less.

Instead of being disillusioned and apathetic about our discoveries of relativity, uncertainty, unpredictability, chance and probability amplitude, we should be happy. It is through these discoveries that we could find the way towards maturity, and a sense of humour. Physics, this pride of humanity, has brought us to a ridiculous position, so let's laugh at ourselves. This ridiculous position is best depicted by the fact that humanity is playing games with the atom, without being able to see or even guess what is going on at the sub-atomic level.

In Robert Oppenheimer's 'Science and Common Understanding', this ridiculous position is evident. One of the fathers of the atomic bomb, he wrote: 'If you ask, for instance, whether the position of the electron remains the same, we must say "no"; if you ask whether the electron's position changes with time, we must say "no"; if you ask whether the electron is at rest, we must say "no"; if you ask whether it is in motion, we must say "no".' These lines give the impression that the electron is mocking us.

In his autobiography, Bertrand Russell explains the following: 'I experienced the delight of believing that the sensible world is real. Bit by bit, chiefly under the influence of physics, this delight has faded' .... 'I find myself involved in a vast mist of solitude, both emotional and metaphysical, from which I can find no issue.'

Obviously there is no issue from a drama for those who like dramas, because drama appeals to their sense of importance. The easiest, and often the only way out of a blind alley is a sense of humour. With a sense of humour we acquire a certain common sense which may tell us that the latest discovery of the quantum theory, that the anti-particles are, in fact, particles moving backward in time, bear no relation to the price of eggs, rheumatism, dentist bills, fear of death, togetherness with our neighbours or our unmarried daughter's pregnancy. Pushed by psychosomatic arousal and restlessness, our scientific explorations have gone way beyond our true needs.

We can mock science because its very essence, its predictability of events, has been mocked by its own achievements: relativity, uncertainty, chance and probability amplitude.

The more we emphasise our self-appointed promotion to the highest position in nature, the more laughable we become. The following passage of Jacques Monod could help take ourselves less seriously: 'We want us to be necessary, inevitable, preordained since eternity. All the religions, almost all the philosophies, even a part of science, bear witness to the heroic, indefatigable effort of mankind to deny in despair its own contingency.'

The only and the easiest way to overcome our contingency is by laughing at it.

ECONOMY AND THE WELFARE STATE

A particularly ridiculous, and seriously damaging, side of our immature way of thinking can be seen in the field of economy.

Individual initiative, personal responsibility, private property, savings and productive investments, these strongholds of the adolescent mentality, all of which found their ideal system in Capitalism, and which noticeably contributed to an increase in the standard of living in a material sense, are slowly disappearing.

What happened? Why did a system like Capitalism, which created such wealth, and improved material conditions for so many, start to become unpopular?

In my opinion, significant changes took place over the last 160 years. Improvement in the standard of living, hygiene, medicine and social assistance, started producing a new humanity, an ever increasing number of old people. This growing element began to change the age structure and the mentality of European society.

We are proud of having nearly doubled our life-span over the last century and a half. With the creation of old age, however, we have brought about a new fear: the fear of old age. Old age has produced a new vulnerability, a vulnerability caused by the feelings of un-selfsufficiency and social dependency. Taking place under emotional arousals caused by fear and vulnerability, the brains' mental activities of the old resulted in a new way of thinking. This new way of thinking produced new art and literature, new philosophy and beliefs, and new theories in politics and economy.

The large number of young who emigrated to America, Australia and other parts of the world has contributed to the increase in the proportion and influence of the old people in Europe.

With the increase in humanitarianism and compassion reflected in Romanticism, a movement originated and perpetuated by this new humanity, another change took place: a rise in the survival of invalids, the chronically sick, the mentally handicapped and the unsuccessful. This un-selfsufficient element joined the un-selfsufficient elderly in their way of thinking.

The longer life-span influenced the minds of many young people. Visualising themselves in old age, they became more aware of their vulnerability which conditioned their mental attitudes.

Longevity also brought the depressing mid-life crises, which in many cases often result in anxiety or despair, these frequent mental disorders of the new humanity.

The dreariness and ugliness of the environment of an industrial society, the asphalt jungle, the claustrophobia in modern cities, urban deracination, traffic congestion, the noise of mechanism in factories, and pollution, all contributed to spreading the old aged mentality among other age groups.

Disillusioned by their expectations, and modern life is open to easy illusions, or frustrated in their pretentions, many young people joined and continue to join the ranks of the new humanity.

A certain number of children born to the new humanity remain handicapped all their lives. The proportion of these children increases with the increase of the new humanity. The number of American babies born with physical or mental defects, for example, has doubled in the last twenty years.

The old-age mental attitude started to firmly establish itself in Europe after the First World War. This new humanity, in fact, won the war. A great number of the young, the healthiest and the fittest element of every European country involved, perished, leaving the crippled, the elderly, the wounded, and those who had wasted the best years of their lives just shooting at each other. Those millions slain left a legacy: the vision of death, an ageing factor in itself.

In my view, one of the main causes of the First World War could well have been the galloping rise of the influence of the new humanity.

The new humanity had started eroding the values of the very foundations of Capitalism and its sacrosanct Nationalistic State.

The European Nationalistic States hoped to solve their internal problems, created by the increasing strength of the new humanity and to regain authority, by external victory. As if spurred on by a death wish, as if they felt that the end of the world was nigh, millions eagerly signed up to be massacred.

It was not the end of the world, however, it was the end of an era, an era ruled by the youthful adolescent mentality. It heralded the beginning of another era, an era which was, is, and will be more and more dominated by the old-age adolescent way of thinking.

Ever since the last world war, nuclear anxiety, particularly among the young, is spreading this old-age attitude, reflected in pacifism or peace movements. The young acquire an old-age frame of mind when they see their future as bleak.

Highly aware of their fragility and their precarious existence, the new humanity drove the adolescent mentality's selfishness and self-centredness to extremes, reaching an 'après moi le déluge' state of mind. This state of mind can be considered a mental disorder, as it consists of a disregard for the species, a disinterest in those who have to continue to live after them. The preservation of the species determines rationality in nature.

With the appearance of the new humanity, many radical changes started taking place.

The new humanity created its own art, an art which was not a reproduction of reality but a reflection of its inner nature. In the guide book of the exhibition in London (1978) of 'Tendencies of the Twenties', one reads: 'Dada and Surrealism are not art movements; they are not even literary movements with attendant artists. They are religions, with a view of the world, a code of behaviour, a hatred of materialism, an ideal of man's future state, a proselytising spirit, a joy in membership of a community of the like-minded, a demand that the faithful must sacrifice other attachments, a hostility to art for art's sake, a hope for transforming existence.'

The new humanity also created its own theatre and literature. These dealt with individual loneliness, hopelessness, finitude, the anxiety of doubt, the rejection of human commitments, and despair.

For centuries laughter had been provoked by 'deformity' as Cicero explained, and by 'infirmity in others', as Hobbes said.

'Renaissance princes collected dwarves, hunchbacks and blackamoors for their merriment', wrote Koestler in his 'Janus', but 'we have become too humane for that kind of fun', he added, omitting to explain why and what kind of humanity lay behind this new humaneness.

Comedies dealing with old people's stubbornness, selfishness and meanness, which used to amuse, slowly disappeared from the stage.

The new humanity created its own philosophy: existentialism. According to this philosophy, human life is meaningless, it is a life in which an involvement is purposeless, any effort hopeless, any sacrifice worthless and any work useles. There is nothing but nothingness.

The brain's mental activity operating under the emotional arousals created by fear of old age or the feeling of unselfsufficiency produced the new humanity's ideal economic system: Socialism. Socialism is a result of the wishful thinking of those who are frightened by their inability to cope with a life of competition and the rat-race of Capitalism.

'Philosophers have only interpreted the world in various ways,' Marx claimed, 'the point, however, is to change it.'

The world did not need Marx to change it. It was already changing. In fact, if it had not been changing, no-one would have ever listened to him.

Marx made a mistake when he stated that a Capitalist society was formed by two social classes fighting each other. It was not two social classes but two different humanities facing each other. In fact, both humanities were bred by individuals belonging to all the social classes of a Capitalist society.

One of the main aims of Socialism was, and still is, to adapt work and social conditions to the new humanity's abilities. The supreme motto of Socialism: 'From each according to his capacities, to each according to his needs,' reflected this aspiration. The disabled, exhausted, disillusioned, chronically ill, unemployed or unemployable, unsuccessful, underprivileged, insecure, or those who are frustrated, incline to invoke a more humane, less competitive, less strenuous economy. This is what Socialism represented and still represents.

It is an established view today that Socialism came into being as a result of the poverty and misery caused by industrialisation. Many historians, however, agree that industrialisation produced more wealth than material misery, and that as a system of production, Capitalism was better equipped to increase the general standard of living than Socialism.

What made the 19th Century so aware of the existing misery? What made other centuries, particularly the 16th and 17th, with their wars and destruction, unaware or uncaring of it?

Extensive misery has existed throughout history, but there were fewer eyes to see it. Only those who suffer notice and participate in the suffering of others. Socialism, with its sentimentality and Romanticism with its sensibility, started together. In fact, the word Socialism was introduced in 1825 at the start of Romanticism.

The new humanity needed sympathy, assistance and protection for its survival. These aspirations found their justification in a powerful abstraction created by the new humanity's mind, that of human dignity. These aspirations inspired the idea of the Welfare State, a state based on the principles of human dignity, compassion and humanitarianism. Democratic Socialism contributed to the creation of the Democratic Welfare States in Western Europe. Through revolution, Communism installed the Totalitarian Welfare States in the East and others parts of the world.

Along the path towards a Welfare State, the Western Democracies adopted the economic policy recommended by a typical representative of the new humanity, John Maynard Keyens (1883-1946). Due possibly to his sexual deviations, and to his 'childless vision', to use Joseph Schumpeter's expression, Keynes created an 'après moi le déluge' economic policy, well suited to the interests and mental disposition of the new humanity. This policy consisted of the State financing the demand and consumption of the present generation at the expenses of the future, a policy of living on credit, and bequeathing to the unborn debts and an 'over-populated desert' to use Ionesco's words.

Keynes' escape from the 'sad reality', ruled by the quantity theory of money, into the euphoria of life on credit and inflation, reflected the new humanity's mental attitude. He gave great pleasure to many when, in 1938, he stated: 'We entirely repudiated a personal liability on us to obey general rules.' His repudiation of the general rules was inspired by the fact that 'in the long run we are all dead,' an idea which helped the 'après moi le déluge' economy, creating a new mental disorder: 'spendomania.'

Keynes' economic policy also contributed to the consolidation of the Welfare States in the West because it increased instability, confused people's planning for the future, and shook confidence in savings, forcing people to rely on the State and its pensions and assistance in their old age.

Obviously both Capitalism and Socialism claim to be superior to each other, each pretending to be more in accordance with human nature. They are both right. Capitalism is in the nature of a humanity which needs competition, and which feels able to cope with life by itself. Socialism is in the nature of a humanity which is unable to survive without help from the State.

The aim of Capitalists is to increase their power and wealth, as these appeal to their egos. The aim of the new humanity, instead, is to improve the quality of life, even if this is achieved, as it often is, at the expense of the material standard of living, as this appeals to its egos.

The Capitalist tries to achieve his aim by sacrificing his life and energy in pursuit of material wealth, whereas the old-age minded tries to achieve his aim by avoiding sacrifices, by working merely to survive.

It makes no sense to claim that Capitalism is superior to Socialism because private industry is more productive than the nationalised industry. The new humanity is aware of this and accept it. Guided by another mental disposition and a different working will and ability, however, they opt for less rigid and less demanding working conditons and better protection of their jobs, which they find in nationalised industry. What is more, in private industry, in search of profit, it is the Capitalist who exploits the workers while in nationalised industry, in search of their own profit, the workers exploit the Capitalist, in other words, the State.

Capitalism gives priority to the production of wealth, and compensation to those who contribute most actively and efficiently to this production. The new humanity gives priority to the distribution of wealth, concentrating this distribution generously and efficiently on the most inactive and unproductive sector of the community. Guided by their humanitarianism, compassion and human dignity, the new humanity does not find any paradox in calling 'social justice' taking wealth from those who work hard and save prudently, in order to compensate those who neither work nor save.

Many critics emphasise that a Welfare State's economy is inefficiently run, but the whole purpose of a Welfare State is to run its economy more humanely. The policy of full employment is not based on economic efficiency but on the principles of humanitarianism, compassion and human dignity.

Individual freedom, innovation, and competition, so glorified by Capitalism, do not appeal to the new humanity which craves to belong and yearns for an easy going co-existence, and fears change.

Many insist that a Welfare State reduces people's eagerness. This is not true. The new humanity is most eager, eager to live with the minimum effort and sacrifice. Every worker in a Welfare State knows his book of rules by heart, and puts all his eagerness into sticking to it, into only working to rule.

'One of the underlying causes of industrial malaise is that people in a Welfare State industry are not motivated any more,' is stressed. The new humanity is highly motivated, but its motives are in accordance with their values: to avoid responsibility and to ensure more leisure-time.

Some experts explain that the productivity of a Welfare State economy is low because of a lack of financial incentives. But experience has proved that any rise in the purchasing power of the new - humanity's salaries or wages, increases not their productivity but their absenteeism and leisure-time.

Many say that people living in a Welfare State are less aggressive and less inventive. On the contrary, they are highly aggressive and most inventive, but only in pursuit of their rights guaranteed by the State. Contrary to a Nationalistic State which emphasises more duties and obligations, a Welfare State is a state of citizens' rights and privileges. The Welfare State introduced the right to public assistance for the unemployed and the unemployable, the right to free medicine and hospital care, the right to free education, the right to paid holidays, the right to child benefits and old-age pensions. These rights are the new wealth, and are as sacrosanct to the new humanity as was the right to private property to Capitalist minded people in the Nationalistic State.

The citizens of a Welfare State, be it in a Democratic or Communist world, take the right to use their office or factory facilities, equipment and materials of their work, for their own personal or private interest, for granted.

Capitalism maintains that savings are the backbone of the economy, but as I have said, the new humanity is not a saving but a consuming humanity. In fact, the new mentality hates those who save. In order to please them, the Welfare State taxes the income from savings higher than that from work.

One of the important assets of a Capitalist economy and its productivity was always considered to be the mobility of the labour force. The old-age minded element, however, are afraid of moving, they fear any new environment.

The new humanity is often accused of a lack of patriotism, particularly when abusing their rights. The old-age minded, however, consider patriotism an exploitative instrument of the Capitalist Nationalistic State. Communist Welfare State workers smile apathetically at their government's slogan: 'Glory of work for the Motherland', which is supposed to increase their productivity.

The new humanity replaced nationalism with trade union solidarity, thus enabling them to exploit the rest of the community and the State more easily.

Marx was wrong when he stressed that the exploitation of men by men belongs to Capitalism. The exploitation of men by men was born with the selfish adolescent mentality. In Communist societies ruled by the old age adolescent mentality, men are even more exploited by men than in Capitalist societies.

The new humanity perpetrated major changes in the nature of law and legal ideology. Inspired by the Welfare State's principles of humanitarianism, compassion and human dignity, justice evolved into equity and fairness. Justice is no longer blind, but ready to see and understand, in order to help, forgive and even to forget. The new justice tends to protect the handicapped, the underprivileged, the under-dog. The judge is less and less the personification of cool and detached severity, of 'lex dura sed lex', and more and more a grand-paternal councellor. The courts are becoming less like solemn forums of justice and more like citizens advisory bureaux.

Slowly but surely, some sooner some later, Democratic Welfare States will end up in Soviet type totalitarian police States. I feel sure that in a hundred years most of the world will live in one form or another of police ruled totalitarian Welfare States.

Why?

Firstly, the population of Democratic Welfare States that are dependent on the State's assistance, increases continuously.

A United Nations study foresees 1,122 million people over the age of 60 in the year 2,025, against the 400 million today. In 1950, the USA and the USSR had 18 million and 16 million 60 year olds and over, respectively. In the year 2,025 the relative figures will be 67 million and 71 million.

By favouring the unfit at the expense of he fit, thereby giving a reproductive advantage to the former, a Democratic Welfare State breeds more and more of its faithful.

In order to face up to the widening gap between its income and its expenses, a Democratic Welfare State is forced to borrow more money on its capital market, leaving less, and on less favourable terms, for productive investment. This jeopardises the future creation of wealth, which reduces the standard of living. This reduced standard of living increases apathy and demoralisation. There is hope that modern electronic technology might help to create the extra wealth needed to support the passive population. This extra wealth, however, may not be sufficient to pay the social benefits of the labour force which will be made redundant by improved technology.

Growing influence in the economy of the Welfare State of unproductive bureaucracy, contributes to the gradual reduction in the standard of living.

In his adolescent way of thinking, ruled by dialectic extremes, Marx did not notice this important social class. He did not foresee their power in Socialism, and above all in Communism, where they cynically exploit State Capitalism on one side, and the masses on the other.

Due to the shabbiness and irresponsibility of the employed new mentality, a Welfare State's economic production lacks quality, thus diminishing quantity thereby contributing to apathy and demoralisation.

In order to pay for the rising needs of the increasing unselfsufficient sector of the community, particularly the 'old-old', those over seventy-five, of which the number is rapidly increasing, (3.2 million in England and Wales, in 1983, compared with 1.7m., in 1951), a Democratic Welfare State is forced to raise the taxation of the working population, gradually pushing them towards more absenteeism and less spontaneous or enthusiastic participation in the production of national wealth.

Faced by the increasing need for more production of wealth, in order to settle the rising bills of this vast number of those in need, on one side, and more and more apathy and absenteeism on the other, a Democratic Welfare State has to introduce some form of forced labour.

With the consolidation of a Welfare State, corruption, crimes against the State's economy and property, parasitism, the abuse of rights and privileges, waste of national wealth due to negligence, absent-mindedness and irresponsibility increase. The rise in dishonesty and crime enforces the State police and its power. A police State is not created by its government, but by its people's crimes. It is the people that deserve the police they have.

Another change which a Democratic Welfare State on its way to a Totalitarian Welfare State carries, is a progressive toughness in the measures and sentences administered for crimes committed against the State economy or its social services. These measures and sentences reach Draconian proportions in a Totalitarian

Welfare State. Those committing crimes against the economy or social services of a State which is based on humanitarianism, compassion and human dignity, are not treated as criminals, but as sinners, as enemies of 'the faith'. They are not punished, therefore, but persecuted until they either repent or perish.

By stressing bad news rather than good, a Democratic Welfare State's media demoralises the atmosphere even more.

In 1977, the British Government advised their national media 'to paint a less gloomy picture, to give more emphasis to successful stories in industry as compared to failures; and to ensure that the failures were reported in a balanced way.' What the British Government did not realise was that the new humanity prefer bad news to good, as bad news justifies their attitude and helps those obsessed by death to depart less painfully from 'a world no longer worth living in.'

The majority of Western Socialists realise that a Soviet type of economy does not work. Why then do they urge their Welfare States towards a Communist form of society?

The pro-Capitalist element are right when they insist that Socialism is 'tragically irrelevant to the future.' Perhaps they are unaware that they are addressing a humanity for whom the future is irrelevant.

Norman Mailer said that 'the function of Socialism is to raise suffering to a higher level.' What he did not explain is that Socialism brings equality of worries and sufferings.

In Totalitarian Welfare States certain capitalist minded people slowly become wealthier than the rest of the community. Periodically, however, they are physically eliminated by some 'cultural revolution' or similar movement inspired by envy. The new humanity cannot stand the inequality.

Many Western politicians claim that everything would change in Soviet Russia if there were free elections.

Fifty million pensioners, millions of alcoholics, a vast number of the chronically lazy, plus the large amount dependent on State assistance might vote for a government of Christian Socialism, for example, which promises the people an even more generous Welfare State. In my view, however, it would only be a question of time before Russia returned to the same Soviet type of Welfare State.

Could this evolution of Democratic Welfare States towards Totalitarian Welfare States be reversed?

From time to time Western Democracies elect a right wing Government who endeavour to change life by reducing the State's interference in the economy, and by the privatisation of nationalised industry. But this is inspired more by nostalgia than by realistic considerations. This can be deduced from any right wing Governments' appreciation and reintroduction of bygone values, rules and principles. These experiments, however, are relatively short in duration, and often cause conditions, such as higher unemployment, which bring the Totalitarian Welfare State nearer.

Between the two World Wars, Fascism in Italy and National Socialism in Germany tried to reverse the trend by imposing an artificially created cult of youthfulness. This consisted of ganging up, noisy ceremonies and colourful marches in the boyish style of old boys or people of the aged mental disposition. Exploiting the emotions created by the glorification of their national past, these two governments over-employed their people in colossal enterprises and grand public works. This merely exhausted them.

Giving importance to formalism, poses, uniforms, class distinction and hypocrisy, Fascism and National Socialism tired them even more.

In their exhaustion and failure to cope with this youthful adolescent idea of super-men, the Fascists and Nazis committed many irrational and arrogant deeds. Perhaps they were provoking the world in search of punishment, longing to relax after the failure of their ideologies.

What then is the future of the Totalitarian Welfare State?

I would like to answer this question with a Russian joke. Two Russians were talking in Moscow.

First Russian: 'What would happen if we installed a Communist State in the Sahara Desert?'

Second Russian: 'For the first fifty years nothing. After that, even the sand would be rationed.'

Sooner or later, a Totalitarian Welfare State must become a State of rationing.

Rationing is the inevitable outcome of social justice based on equality and humanitarianism, coupled with a persistent deficit between the demand for goods and services, and their supply.

Many Totalitarian Welfare States try to postpone rationing merely to save face. This introduces that 'popular' occupation, queueing. People queue for goods and services at the expense of productive activities. Queueing is also demoralising which consolidates the Totalitarian Welfare State.

With the growing increase in the passive population, and the progressive decrease in the active element, slowly but surely, a Totalitarian Welfare State reaches the critical ratio between those living on State assistance and those working for it, a situation in which the working population cannot provide enough food and services to keep themselves alive, let alone the passive population as well. This is when, in the name of humanitarianism, a Totalitarian Welfare State starts rationing the needy, thereby eliminating the most expensive minority in the community. Before long it could be against the law to have more than one child, or even any at all. One must keep in mind that such legislation would be in tune with the 'après moi le déluge' mentality.

The Totalitarian Welfare State's media has no trouble convincing those who survive that the elimination of 'social parasites' is in their interest. In some Totalitarian Welfare States the principle of the eradication of these parasites has already been established. For the moment the principle is only valid for domestic pets. State propaganda has already invented slogans easily adaptable in the future for the liquidation of human social parasites.

'We should kill pets for public good. These animals need feeding, they serve no real purpose. Their food is needed for humans or for productive animals,' the slogans scream. 'It is a bourgeois indulgence to have pets,'... 'The sacrifice of pets must be done in the public interest.'...There are many people in certain countries who prefer their pets to their children.

The human species may well be eliminated, but not in a nuclear holocaust as is the popular belief, but in the progressive elimination of ever-increasing social parasites by an ever-decreasing working population.

In my view, however, at the end of its tether, the Totalitarian Welfare State should bring about the collapse of the ruling adolescent mentality, and the beginning of a more intelligent life inspired by maturity, by a common sense mentality.

Throughout history there is evidence that whenever men's ideologies, beliefs and speculations fall into decadence, women resumed prominence. This is a natural reaction because, when confused and demoralised, men return to infancy. In moments of crisis, women acquire natural maturity which is impregnated with humaneness.

There is a big difference between men's humanitarianism and women's humaneness. Men invented humanitarianism in order to exploit it; in fact, man mainly practises it at the expense of others. Women's humaneness, however, is inbuilt, and is exercised at their own expense. It is an integral part of maturity which implies fruitfulness.

The mature mentality will take over as soon as the present young and old adolescent mentalities sink to the lowest level, a level of utter folly. At this level, their arrogance and aggression will have to vanish, allowing common sense with its joy of living to emerge from inhibition and oppression. This will trigger off liberation and the revival of many people's dormant or hidden maturity.

In spite of centuries of ideological and religious indoctrination under the adolescent mentality's culture, and in spite of this culture's insistence that the present values, style of life and way of thinking belong to humanity as a whole, there are still many mature people around. In their maturity, however, they consider it wise to adapt to the existing way of life. They find it prudent not to provoke the arrogance, aggression, selfishness and self-centredness of the ruling adolescent mentality with either common sense or their sense of humour. In the present atmosphere, mature women are not only inhibited in their common sense way of reasoning by the male adolescent mentality, but also by so-called liberated women who imitate the male adolescent mental attitude.

Maturity cannot overthrow the adolescent mentality with rebellion. Rebellions and revolutions are not in the nature of maturity; besides, maturity lacks aggression. The only way, therefore for maturity to replace the present young and old adolescent mentalities is when the latter sink to the laughing point of no return. Perhaps the recent rush towards catastrophe reflects the adolescent mentality's desire to reach this level of existence as soon as possible in order to return to the relaxed innocence of infancy or to advance towards the serenity of maturity.

In a common sense atmosphere, the revival of the adolescent mentality would be more difficult, as in a common sense atmosphere, a sense of humour with its derision of pretentiousness, rules supreme. In a mature mentality world, it would soon be realised that ideologies only seduce egomaniacs by promising them the domination of reality. People would see that ideologies always end up in what Marx called 'revolution in permanence', a pathetic nightmare in which a stubborn believer tries to recover his increasing loss in the fight against nature. Above all, people will realise that both Capitalism, which appeals to the youthful adolescent mentality, and Socialism, which is in tune with the old-minded adolescent mentality, are irrelevant to the problems of modern life. Capitalism creates problems and then insists that it alone can solve the problems it has created. Socialism does the same. What is more, any doctrinaire's cure of a problem produces side effects which are far more damaging than the problem itself.

In a climate of maturity, filled with the joy of living, an adolescent minded individual will not need to search for an escape from the 'sad' reality into the promises of ideologies. He will discover that he is not lonely or isolated any more, as maturity's fruitfulness and yielding create an atmosphere of participation and togetherness. The mind of an individual does not need to fantasise when he belongs to a community. He no longer feels threatened by life. When threatened, we incline to be seduced by fantasies and illusions.

People will take any attempt to revive the adolescent mentality as a joke, because they will remember this mentality's achievements, well stressed by Sakharov, the Nobel prize winner for peace, and which will be engraved in public places. 'Civilisation is imperiled by: a universal nuclear war,' he said, 'is imperiled by catastrophic hunger for most of mankind, stupefaction from narcotics of "mass culture" and bureaucratised dogmatism, a spreading of mass myths that put entire peoples and continents under the power of cruel and treacherous demagogues, consequences of swift changes in the conditions of our planet.'

In an atmosphere impregnated by maturity, an adolescent will lose his rebelliousness. Being unable to hide behind conceit, or to escape into his ideologies for fear of derision, an adolescent feels naked, and a nude is seldom aggressive.

With humanity ruled by a mature mentality, a Welfare State could work and prosper. It would not be conditioned by humanitarianism, compassion and the adolescent human dignity, but by humaneness, shame and a mature human dignity.

In a world dominated by maturity, shame will discourage people from exploiting the community and the State, and from abusing individual rights and privileges. Shame will save an enormous amount of national resources by preventing or eliminating waste.

The third strong pillar of the new Welfare State would be mature human dignity. In the adolescent mentality's Welfare State, human dignity serves as a kind of beggar's right or entitlement to the exploitation of the State. In maturity, human dignity is a state of benevolence, an incentive to build the community and its dignity.

In an atmosphere dominated by maturity, a Welfare State can work and prosper because, above all, people in maturity develop a love for work. In maturity, work relieves the itch which is generated and perpetuated by the fruitfulness and fecundity carried by maturity.

This love of work, an integral part of maturity, bears no resemblance to the Puritan Protestants' work ethic. An ethic inspires self-righteousness, which, being aggressive, frightens the new humanity.

It is important to note that in ancient cultures when women were in prominence (Egypt, Crete, Rome) work was respected and loved, whereas where women were treated as slaves and inferior to men (Greece and Europe in the Middle Ages) work was considered as base, tiring and humiliating. Love of work, in fact, is one of the main characteristics of woman's maturity. Man acquires love of work in his maturity because, when he reaches it, he acquires the maternal mentality.

This need for work would consolidate the new Welfare State

for a major reason. With the love of work, the quality of production increases, improving the quality of life, the joy of living and mature human dignity.

In a world ruled by maturity, Judeo-Christianity will become a laughing matter. Created by the adolescent mentality, it invented that work was a punishment.

After all, Judeo Christianity is out of date. It was invented when the human life-span was around thirty-five years.

A recent survey by the United Nations shows that Judeo-Christianity is still influencing our egos. In the USA, only 52 percent of the occupied population are happy in their work, compared with 45 percent in Sweden, 26 percent in Germany and 17 percent in Great Britain.

Schools do not prepare us to like work, or to build a life of contentment with the love of work. We are thought to be obsessed with success, with winning. The irony is that these aims are never reached. It is in the nature of those in pursuit of success or victory to want more, and 'more' kills 'enough', in which one can find contentment and happiness.

In an atmosphere where work was enjoyed the organisation of labour would change. More and more work would take place in the home. Using home as one's work-shop would help consolidate the family.

A community ruled by a common sense maturity could provide a better economy for another major reason: the disappearance of envy. Envy belongs to the adolescent mentality.

The mature mentality realises that inequality is a natural law, and considers it beneficial for the survival of the human species in a life ruled by relativity, unpredictability, uncertainty and chance.

It was the new humanity that created the idea of equality in the name of which they passionately opposed natural inequality among humans. To those aware of their inadequacy, inequality was unacceptable as to them it implied superiority and inferiority. In the world of maturity, however, inequality merely means differences among people, and this does not offend, particularly when it is realised that individual differences are good for the community and the species.

In a Welfare State ruled by maturity, Socialism's motto: 'From each according to his capacities, to each according to his needs,' will finally make sense. This thoughtful Socialist policy never works in a system based on equality.

In inventing this generous motto, the Socialists must have been inspired by nostalgia for their infancy, a happy state of existence organised by the mother and her love, as well as her inborn sense of fairness. In fact, only a mother can guess her children's, and, by intuition or reasoning analogy, other people's individual capacities and needs, and transform the Socialist motto into a working policy.

Reaching maturity, humanity could finally use their brains intelligently and to the full extent. We are proud of our brain, enormous in relation to the size of the body, but, alas, we never use more than 20-30 percent of its capacity. This reduced activity of the brain is mainly due to the emotional arousals created and perpetuated by the adolescent mind's self-created fears. With his adolescent mentality, man is not 'Homo sapiens', but 'Homo credulus'. 'Homo credulus' cannot think properly because he is trembling on the brink of a precipice, hanging onto his wishful beliefs.

With a greater use of our brain we may find a comic side to the basic theories of Capitalism and Communism in the essential field of economy, that of the factors of production.

Capitalism insists that capital is the essential factor of production and value; Communism, however, gives total priority to labour. Considering labour as the one and only factor of production and value, Communism aims to 'contradict' capital, to denigrate its prepotence and aggression and to eliminate its threat.

They are both wrong. To the common sense reasoning, capital and labour are not the factors but the instruments of production. They can both be productive and create value and plus-value in the hands of an efficient and productive organisation, but a minus value in the hands of an inefficient organisation. In their dogmatic attitudes, neither Capitalism nor Communism could have seen the importance of the actual organisation in the creation of wealth. They cannot see the importance of the organisation because they both live by beliefs, and beliefs imply aggression which is the negation of a real organisation. Being rational and pragmatic, organisation belongs to maturity, to a maternal mentality.

In the present phase of doctrinal beliefs, the organisation in Capitalist and Communist Welfare States ends in the hands of the most inefficient element: bureaucracy.

There is another ridiculous side to Capitalism and Communism. Capitalism's supreme aim, 'the greatest happiness of the greatest number' is incongruous. It is impossible for an individual to achieve happiness without belonging to a happy community. But, there is no happy community where all individuals, often unscrupulously, are pursuing their own personal happiness. On the other hand, Communism creates a paradox: happiness in the equality of unhappiness.

Perhaps, however, the adolescent way of thinking could fade out without reaching apocalyptic levels, by reforming the policy making bodies. Parliaments in Democratic Welfare States, and Politbureaux in Totalitarian Welfare States should introduce an important innovation. Between the ranks separating the Government Party and the Opposition in Democratic Welfare State Parliaments, and among the members of Totalitarian Welfare State Politbureaux, a group of popular humourists should have permanent seats. Their mere presence would shake the doctrinaire self-confidence of the politicians, opening their eyes to common sense reality. Instead of emphasising their differences, differences often of a purely speculative nature, with common sense, the quarrelling politicians might find many positive things in common, all good for their community.

The humourists should concentrate particularly on the extreme left-wing, as they play their power game with the emotions of the highly vulnerable new humanity. The humourists would have an easy task with these popular demagogues as they could show that many of them are Capitalists at heart. In fact, when in power these politicians enjoy a life of luxury and opulence, treating their dependents and the community like any cool, detached Capitalist exploiter.

The presence of the humourists in the decision making bodies would perform miracles, as politicians dread derision even more than losing elections, and this is saying a lot.

Being closer to nature, therefore less intoxicated by abstractions, over-seriousness or ideologies, certain so-called primitive tribes in Africa use humour when they realise that the discussion cannot provide the solution to litigation or an argument. They also replace their Chieftans when they have been successfully derided.

Ever since Ancient Egypt and Persia, up until the French Monarchy, humourists, in various forms, played an important role. They were representatives of common sense, a great help to rulers isolated from reality. With their sense of humour, these 'buffoons' helped in softening or questioning 'The Right Divine of Kings to govern wrongly,' as Alexander Pope said.

I feel certain that the world would be in better shape if, whether in Washington or in the Kremlin, there was more sense of humour and less over-seriousness.

AGGRESSION

With a sense of humour reasoning, we might see the pathetic side of our destructive aggression.

There are two main views regarding the origin of man's aggression. To Instinctivists our aggressiveness is phylogenetically programmed, an instict. For this school of thought, life is a jungle in which the fittest, whatever that may mean, has a better chance of survival and of transmitting his aggressive genes to the following generations. To Behaviourists, human aggression is mainly caused by social and cultural environments.

There is even a tendency to link these two extremes by explaining that our aggressiveness is a result of the interaction of our environments, with inherited genes.

These theories are in accord with the adolescent mentality, a mentality which seeks to excuse an individual's selfish and self-centred behaviour, Instinctivists blaming nature, Behaviourists blaming environment.

Some representatives of the instinct theory claim that our aggression is highly beneficial. In his book 'On Aggression', Konrad Lorenz wrote: 'Summing up what has been said in this chapter, we find that aggression, far from being the diabolic destructive principle that classical psychoanalysis makes it out to be, is really an essential part of life, preserving the organisation of instincts.'

In Spengler's 'Man and Techniques', we read the following: 'The beast of prey is the highest form of active life ... The human race ranks highly because it belongs to the class of the beast of prey' ... 'the life of a man is the life of a brave and splendid, cruel and cunning beast of prey. He lives by catching, killing and consuming. Since he exists he must be master.'

In Bertrand Russell's 'Authority and the Individual', we read: 'The old instincts that have come down to us from our tribal ancestors, all kinds of aggressive impulses inherited from generations of savages' ...

I would like to point out to those who insist that man was and is a born 'hunter and killer', that nature would never have given the predatory instinct to a species with the digestive system of a vegetarian, like other primates. If man was a 'beast of prey' he would never have started agriculture, the domestication of animals and the dairy industry.

There might be a clearer understanding of the subject if we analysed the origin and nature of the energy that is needed for human aggressiveness to materialise.

As I have explained, the brain and the nervous system of both animals and humans are programmed to increase the energy in their bodies in cases of emergency such as when they have to defend their survival or the survival of their offspring and when they have to satisfy their needs inspired by biological discomforts, such as hunger, thirst and sex. In nature, aggression is either a defence against an objective threat, or a reaction to fears caused by physiological imbalance or discomfort. In both cases the extra energy is provided by biological arousals created by real fears.

Humans, however, also possess the mind's generated aggression which is offensive.

Offensive aggressiveness is mainly inspired by our inflated ego's fear of failure.

Like a realistic danger to physical survival, any positive or imaginary threat to our ego, or to the survival of our mind's world, creates an emergency state of existence. In emotional arousals, produced by this state of emergency, offensive aggressiveness finds the energy which helps its materialisation, the energy for its destructiveness.

Why is offensive aggression destructive?

Because the main threat to the adolescent mind's ego and its imaginary world is nature, objective reality. There is only one way to protect our mind's world against nature and that is by changing it to please our mind. Moulding nature to suit the wishful abstractions of our mind results in destroying nature.

Neither Instinctivists nor Behaviourists realise the strength of the mind, or the aggression inspired by it. Our mind's infatuations, prejudices and beliefs are far stronger than our genes or environment. Our physical self-preservation is secondary to the preservation of our inflated ego.

Some people attribute human offensive aggression, violence and crimes to the 'bestial' in us. This 'brutality' of our nature would lie in our unconscious, and the unconscious world would also provide an anarchic energy needed to realise these brutalities. We are lucky, however, these people insist, because our conscious is able to restrain this 'demonic' potential of our unconscious, to refer to an idea of Kierkegaard, or to control 'wild dogs howling in the cellar', to quote Nietzsche's vision of our unconscious.

The energy for our so-called animal behaviour is not produced by some mysterious well in our dark unconscious, but by our mind's created arousal. Neither the unconscious nor instincts can play a role in human offensive and destructive aggression for the simple reason that most crimes and atrocities are premeditated.

The mind's created imagination, prejudices, beliefs or calculations play an essential part in premeditation.

The following facts could help in proving that the origin of our destructive aggression lies in our minds.

Ablation of the frontal lobe where the wishful way of thinking seems to take place, reduces offensive aggressiveness.

Offensive aggression can be manipulated by influencing the mind with propaganda or brainwashing.

In order to arouse aggressiveness in their followers, political and military leaders depict their opponents as monsters, criminals or dangerous war-mongers. Conflicts are carried on by the energy provided by fears of defeat, and fears of defeat by 'monsters' increase emotional arousals and aggression even more.

Hysterical delirium of the masses, created by the manipulation of their minds, can lead to the most atrocious destruction and savagery.

Superstitions, ideologies and religions are among the main sources of offensive aggression.

When the mind becomes obsessed by a belief or an idea, it develops fanaticism, a serious cause of destruction.

Tyranny, this epitome of offensive aggression, is always based on an ideology.

One of the worst types of offensive aggression can be found in persecutions or revolutions, and these are inspired by an idea or a belief.

Other major instigators of crime and violence are racial or national prejudices, all creations of the mind. People inspired by these prejudices often justify their killings with the belief that they are not eliminating members of their own species, other human beings, but 'barbarians' or 'Undermenschen'.

Jealousy, envy, vanity, resentment, malice, despise and spitefulness are all sources of offensive aggression, and are all states of mind, or emotions created by states of mind.

'There is no love without aggression,' stressed Lorenz. This is very true, but only in those with the adolescent mentality. Their love, in fact, is self-love, and this is aggressive.

Throughout time and space, the torture of man by man has been committed in the name of a belief or a prejudice. Inquisitors are always ardent believers.

Man considers a moral insult a good reason for strongreaction. But insults stem from excessive self-esteem.

Some people insist that frustration is at the root of most of our offensive aggression. Frustration, however, is nothing but self-infatuation offended by reality. We are frustrated in a bus or train full of what we consider ugly and ordinary people, or working in a crowded office or factory. We are not frustrated, however, by a much bigger gathering at a reception at Buckingham Palace or the White House, or a fashionable night club. Man is seldom frustrated by the crowd in which he feels important, that is applauding him, carrying him on their shoulders or pressing him for his autograph.

Self-confidence is another significant source of destructive aggression. It finds its energy in the gap between individual pretentiousness and feelings of inadequacy.

The glorification of self-confidence invaded Western Europe with the Renaissance. 'It is better to be adventurous than cautious,' wrote Machiavelli, 'because fortune is like a woman, and if you wish to keep her under, it is necesary to beat and ill-use her.' Machiavelli certainly did not know that self-confidence in a life ruled by uncertainty and unpredictability ends in a stubborness derided by ironies. Corneille was much wiser when, in his 'Cid' he explained that 'Danger breeds best on too much confidence.'

There is one particular field in which human destructive aggressiveness likes to materialise itself, the field of art. (I will use the word art in reference to what are known as 'fine arts'.)

In art man assumes the role of Almighty God, the role of creator. After all, creating man 'after his own image and likeness', God endowed him with a 'creative drive'.

What is art?

Art is an act of creation from nothingness, a work of the imagination, a novelty in nature, or to be more precise: a novelty against nature.

What drives an artist towards the creation of a novelty?

The answer could be the artist's discontent with reality, his fear of real life. In fact, it is an emotional arousal generated by this fear that provides the artist with his creative ideas. An artist's imaginative speculations and visualisations are in essence the result of his brain's incomplete or poor mental activity operating under pressure caused by high fears or strong feelings of inadequacy or vulnerability. With their higher fears or stronger feelings of inadequacy or vulnerability, individuals belonging to a minority group in a society tend to be more endowed with artistic creativity and imagination than individuals belonging to the majority.

We live in laughable times. Our present culture considers artistic creations fashioned with a diminished mental activity and with reduced efficiencies of our sensory system and perceiving mechanism as valuable. We are proud of paying enormous prices for painting or sculptures representing distorted life perceived by an artist's inadequate perception. We applaud the works of Brecht or Beckett instead of feeling sorry for their authors. We should pity them because they were unable to see the beautiful side of life. They were unable to see the beautiful side of life because in their self-infatuations they lived a life of high emotional arousals which, in their cases, produced a desparate way of thinking.

An artist is not usually inspired by poetic nobility or lyrical humaneness, but by a capricious desire to replace the real world which does not please his ego with his own world in which he feels omnipotent, in which he is dominant. Most artists, in fact, believe that they have a high calling to change the world in the name of their inspirations, visions or revelations, all of which are the results of the brain's incomplete mental activity produced by high emotional arousals, caused by the strong fears of inflated egos.

An artist's creation, therefore, ends up by annihilating reality, and transforming live nature into still life. 'In scorn of nature, art gave lifeless life,' Shakespeare explained in his 'The Rape of Lucrece'.

Plato banished artists from his idealised City-State, from his poetic world. Creators fear each other.

Being a materialisation of an artist's aggressiveness, thus a symbol of aggression or intimidation, works of art inspire fears.

People living in a higher precariousness of their abstract worlds are more inclined to perceive and be attracted by a work of art, as they are more easily frightened by any sign of offensive aggression. One can only be impressed by a work of art if frightened by it, if threatened by its message.

We are told that confronted with a work of art we get emotionally involved. It is not explained, however, how we got this emotion in the first place, how this emotion came into existence. In order to get emotionally involved, there must be an emotion.

This emotion is nothing but arousal caused by fear of the artist's creation. Obviously this is best shown in grotesque or macabre forms of art, or art representing a twisted or tormented world, much spread by expressionism and surrealism.

Significant evidence that artistic creations are offensively aggressive is that people discharge their fear of them into laughter if the creations are a failure.

Above all, we can deduce that a work of art is an act of aggression by the fact that it can give us goose-pimples, sweaty palms, widening of the pupils, warmth over the body, blushing, and an increase in our pulse rate. These are also all reactions we experience when confronted with danger.

We consider emotional arousals caused by the fear of artistic creations as positive emotions if they please our ego, but negative if they do not. With the same arousal we can find beauty or ugliness in a work of art. Beauty and ugliness are in the mind of the beholder. Ugliness is what frightens our mind, beauty that which pleases it. We can beautify ugliness when we tame it or when we overcome our inital fear of it.

We can overcome our initial fear of art by learning about it, by becoming familiar with it. Our knowledge of the perceived artistic creation can transform the inital arousal created by the fear of it into a pleasant emotion. An emotional arousal caused by the fear of a work of art becomes a pleasant emotion because our understanding of it and our critical judgement of it flatters our ego, as they produce a sense of victory over fear.

There is another fact which makes us like the arts in spite of their aggression.

As our culture has indoctrinated us to recognise works of art as highly valuable, and their appreciation a sign of intellectual or aesthetic superiority, we consider the emotional arousal caused by the perception of these works as a positive and pleasant emotion.

Many people decorate their houses with works of art. They like to surround themselves with them as it makes them feel as if they are living more intensely. The emotional arousals produced by the fear of these works, particularly if they are well-known and expensive, please the people's egos.

Certain unstable people can reach exaltation or ecstasy confronted by artistic creations. Frightened by them, they escape to even higher levels of their mind's fantasies, into a partial or total insensitivity.

Being more susceptible to fear, men are more artistically minded than women. Many women who are not affected by the male mentality, smile at men's efforts to impress each other with their artistic creations or possessions.

The offensive aggression of an art against nature and its order and harmony can best be seen in music.

Any sound in nature, perceived by a living being, alerts him. A sound alerts animals and humans because it is an external sign of the emotional arousals provoked by fears, sufferings or biological discomfort. Both animals and humans fear those who are frightened.

If natural sounds alert humans and animals, man's artifically created music alerts both even more. It would be more accurate to consider that animals were more bemused than amused by Orpheus' lute. A snake charmer does not charm the snake, but confuses the nature of it by the noise of his instrument. We all know that sudden loud noises can paralyse.

We are well aware that noises are intimidating because we raise our voice whenever we intend to frighten.

When we are lost, particularly in the dark, we often sing in order to intimidate whatever the darkness is hiding.

Many people at pop festivals, or even when just listening to taped music, sometimes have convulsions, crying and tearing at their hair. These are all signs of fear, and the energy to exteriorise these signs is related to the emotional arousals caused by the fear of the music they are listening to.

The emotional tension of people at a concert of classical music or an opera can be sensed. The emotional arousal provoked by a musical performance is discharged like a volcanic eruption into frenzied applause, spasmodic ovation often accompanied by orgasmic screams, at the end of a successful musical or operatic performance.

With this applause and ovation the audience is mainly showing its relief that the performance is over. The arousal caused by classical music is considered a positive emotion because our culture has indoctrinated us that it is distinguished to appreciate it. In reality, people often only attend concerts and the opera to satisfy their egos, not their ears.

Some adolescents spend hours listening to the loudest pop music and consider the arousal caused by it an enjoyable positive emotion because their fear of the music helps them to escape from reality which, in their conceit, they find dreary.

By persevering in listening to music certain people who are oversensitive to fear, can fall into a trance. This is the result of a strongly reduced brain's mental activity caused by the increasing fear produced by the persisting music.

We find some sounds of nature, like those of certain birds or rivers in the countryside, pleasant and relaxing. This happens when, through experience, we have learnt that behind those sounds there lies no threat. We fear and consider unpleasant, however, the arousal caused by sounds such as thunder, guns, or the roar of a lion, as they herald potential peril.

It could be argued that if my theory was true, why do we sing lullabys to babies to calm them and send them to sleep. In my view, it is not the singing that lulls them, but our presence and nearness that reassures them.

We listen to music early in the morning to help increase our arousal which helps us to wake up. We play music at work to enhance our nervous energy, thereby improving our performance. We apply music to animals in order to increase their productivity, but this only succeeds if they are enclosed. If the animals or birds were free they would flee from the noise.

We use particularly loud music accompanied often with shouts in order to raise people's arousals and aggressivity, necessary in battle or combat.

There is a great fallacy perpetuated by our present culture that the arts ennobled humanity, making it gentler, kinder, or more civilised.

Throughout history, however, many of the world's worst criminals were either artistically creative or admirers of the arts.

Periods of the most atrocious crimes and violence, such as the Fifth century B.C. in Greece, and the Fifteenth and the Sixteenth centuries in the rest of Europe, coincided with the prosperity of artistic creativities.

The Ancient Greeks knew only too well that offensive aggression and the arts were intimately connected when they placed the goddess Athena protector of them both. They also knew that aggression and the arts were products of the mind's self-infatuation and self-created omnipotence when they claimed that Athena came out of Zeus's head. 'At the stroke of the bronze-heeled axe, Athena sprung from the height of her father's head with a strong cry. The sky shivered before her and earth our mother too.'

It is interesting to note that in his 'Eumenides', Aeschylus attributed the following proud statement to Athena: 'No mother bore me, in all things my heart turns to the male, save only for wedlock, and I incline wholly to the father.'

Athena, the supreme goddess of men's offensive aggression, and of their fine arts, was therefore the daughter of a male. She had no mother.

What is the answer to this destructive aggression?

There is only one way to eliminate the adolescent mentality's offensive aggression, and that is the debasement of its source, its source being the ideological or idealised abstract world of the mind, and the best way of debasing the adolescent mind is by self-derision.

Recently we have been aiding and abetting the most humourous scene. We listen to loud complaints that the world is going to the dogs, that beliefs and idologies are in a crisis, that mental confusion rules supreme and that scepticism is increasing.

But in fact, this is perhaps the best news that humanity could hope for. In my opinion, it is a big step towards common sense and maturity.

Beliefs and ideologies are in a crisis simply because they can no longer be realised.

Countries which used to force their wishful beliefs onto reality with their armies and weapons can no longer do this. They would have to resort to nuclear arms against those also in possession of nuclear arms. Our nuclear era had produced the first deriding blow to the adolescent dialectical way of thinking, based on the contradiction of opposites. After all, it must be ridiculous to use the victor/victim way of thinking in a nuclear age.

Perhaps we should be thankful for nuclear arms, as they may help us to pass from adolescence into maturity. They could even be a blessing in disguise as they could force humanity to reason before fantasising.

LONELINESS

I would like to expose another of our absurd achievements: loneliness.
Loneliness starts with adolescence and is carried into later years by the adolescent mentality. Children and mature people are seldom lonely because the former have play, the latter their fruitfulness and generosity.
Encouraging individual independence, especially in Western culture, created and continues to create aloneness in which many people develop fear and anxiety, producing feelings of loneliness. The independence and autonomy of individuals goes against togetherness and the community, which makes them isolated, miserable and unhappy. In their independence and autonomy, people feel lonely and frightened because it is not in the nature of our species to be independent. We are a group species in which an individual's survival and happiness depends on the community. Our species has the longest infancy and old age, making us more dependent on the community than any other species.
Many people's supreme aim is individual independence but, the nearer they reach their goal, the lonelier they feel, and the more they long to belong.
J. J. Rousseau seduced millions by insisting that in a state of nature man was free.
In his Romanticism, Rousseau did not realise that nowhere is man less free than in a state of nature. In a state of nature he is ruled by the laws of natures. Freedom of the individual really

means freedom from nature, from reality, and above all freedom from responsibility towards his community. Rousseau, in fact, abandoned his children to the care of others.

We invented individual freedom in order to rise above nature, but the world above nature and reality is a world of isolation and loneliness, a world of fears.

Individual freedom implies freedom of choice, an amusing phenomenon created by the human mind.

Analysing the origin of the bio-energy needed for freedom of choice, and of the bio-energy needed to keep choice alive, we may discover that freedom of choice is an illusion, the result of a restricted way of thinking.

Being an unnatural activity, freedom of choice needs extra bio-energy to materialise itself.

I have explained that extra bio-energy can be provided by extra fears.

What kind of fears create the bio-energy needed for freedom of choice, and for standing by that choice?

The bio-energy needed to choose one thing instead of its opposite is provided by a fear of its opposite. Before an actual choice between two polarised positions takes place, there has to be a wishful idea. A wishful idea conjures up an idea of its opposite which produces fears, fears which originate the bio-energy needed to materialise the wishful idea. Any realisation of a wishful idea or belief, which we call a free choice, in essence aims at the elimination of the opposite. But, this is a futile effort. The menacing opposites cannot be eliminated until the wishful ideas or beliefs are in existence.

Freedom of choice is unknown in human maturity. As in nature, ruled by natural laws, in maturity's reasoning, ruled by common sense logic, there is no freedom of choice. Truth is not free.

The adolescent way of thinking feels free because its roots waver in the fantasies of the mind. The mature way of reasoning is not free because its roots are firmly in the ground.

Behind our so-called free choice lie our mind's created fears. We have the impression that we vote freely in a free election. We seldom realise, however, that the energy and determination to vote for a certain political party is provided by the fear of the success of the opposition.

Even the most trivial everyday choice is a fear-inspired decision.

Many people advise that the lonely should be encouraged to acquire self-confidence. Self-confidence, however, creates even more isolation and loneliness. Self-confidence is not really confidence in owns self, but merely in our self-opinionated ego. Helping and re-assuring people's self-opinionated egos, can only drive them deeper into exile from reality, therefore into more loneliness.

Certain organisations have recently been trying to teach the lonely 'the art of being assertive'. Trying to teach lonely self-opinionated people how to be assertive will only make them lonelier as everyone will avoid them.

Culture, colour, class and race differences are all blamed for people's loneliness, but these are only a barrier to those who consider their position to be superior or inferior to the others in their bracket, thereby creating their own particular loneliness.

Feeling hurt by the external world can also create loneliness, but it is usually the unfulfilled expectations of our ego that hurt. A self-precious ego is highly susceptible to all manner of offence and humiliation.

Some people explain that their loneliness is due to their unworthiness. Those martyrs who are so obsessed with their self-importance often think themselves unworthy because they find very little to do that they consider worthy of their conceited ego.

Loneliness implies free time in which to be lonely, in which to wallow in self-pity. Using some of this free time for the sake of others leaves less time for loneliness and self-pity. Everyone can help someone.

Some people blame their parents or society in general for their loneliness. In their selfishness and self-centredness, these spoilt people consider that they are entitled to their rights from their parents and society, without any obligations.

Many people attribute loneliness to lack of communication. By nature, apart from the physically handicapped, we are endowed with the ability to communicate. Many lonely people are lonely not because of their inability to communicate, but due to a desperate search for a form of communication that satisfies their inflated egos. Such inflated egos seldom find communications which they consider worthwhile.

Shyness is often blamed for loneliness.

What is it that makes people shy?

An individual's awareness of the gap between his inflated ego and his real self is one of the main causes of his fear of social clumsiness, fear of the failure of his ego, and fear of being ridiculed by reality, which we call shyness, and which makes him dread commitments or involvements.

Shyness is a kind of protective shield for those who cannot reconcile themselves to what they really are.

Helping to escape from reality, shyness, for a short time, can even be a pleasant emotion. Carrying fear, an escape can trigger off the release of the brain's opiates which produce a temporary pleasure. Like all pleasures, shyness can become an addiction, and like all pleasures, it can kill the joy of living. Loneliness prospers in post pleasure melancholia or depression.

Being afraid of loneliness, we face the problem with a certain emotional arousal, therefore with a reduced reasoning which can neither solve nor cure the problem.

Consisting of suffering in aloneness, loneliness can be considered a mental disorder, and like any mental disorder it finds its origin in the mind's created selfishness or self-centredness. Like the selfishness of other mental disorders, the selfishness of the lonely is of an instant nature, a here and now selfishness. Like any other mental disorder, loneliness is the sufferer's creation, his own responsibility. As in other mental disorders, the lonely make their own misery by taking themselves too seriously.

Excessive loneliness can result in a serious mental disorder, persecution mania. The greatest champion of individual freedom and independence, Rousseau, ended his life in madness, imagining plots against him, constantly repeating: 'Everyone hates me'.

A Welfare State ruled by maturity should organise courses in a sense of humour, above all for those approaching old age, those who are most susceptible to loneliness. These old people could learn how to take themselves less seriously, how to develop self-ridicule and tease each other. There, they could also be taught how to age in the most beneficial way, beneficial both to themselves and the community. Anyone can integrate himself into the community simply by learning how to ingratiate himself with it. By developing a sense of self-ridicule, people acquire charm.

A sense of humour could help lonely old people in one of the most invigorating manifestations: smiling.

Facial expressions are infectious producing in those who perceive them the emotion behind them. In fact, the gloomy face of an old person spreads a certain unease, often an unhealthy sense of guilt.

The old can contribute to the community by expressing their gratitude and their appreciation of society's help, by smiling. Brought on by gratitude or appreciation, a smile is the expression of a state of innocence and this inspires generosity in others.

These courses should also advise the old, and those approaching old-age, to re-learn how to play. 'There are toys for all ages,' as an English saying goes. In learning how to play, these people would find togetherness and therefore be less lonely. By learning how to play, they would also be able to avoid the time-wasting psychiatrist's couch, or the gloom of the Church. There is much truth in an Italian proverb which reads: 'Whoever is playing is confessing'.

After these courses many people would realise the following facts: that an individual can only solve his problem of loneliness or unhappiness through a community; that a community can only be built by the individual's participation in it; that there is no participation without contribution.

These courses should also explain that maturity's fruitfulness and fecundity either means contributing more to the community than one takes from it, or being grateful if one has received more than one has contributed. People with the adolescent mentality are never grateful or appreciative. They pay for this by their loneliness.

INTERPERSONAL RELATIONSHIPS

Many people claim that there is a serious problem today in our interpersonal relationships and communications. This problem, however, has existed since the adolescent revolution.

For millions of years we lived as a community species. These communities, composed of inter-dependent members, were formed either around mothers or the older females. It is in the nature of children, and of the neotonous male to seek protection and guidance from mother figures.

As I have explained, those male adolescents who were unable or unwilling to adapt to the natural order of the community, were left behind or rejected by it. When these loose bachelors gathered together, they formed a gang, a collectivity which was an association of equal individuals acting in concert, inspired by the same idea and guided by the same belief.

With the adolescent revolution, the collectivity, formed by these bachelors, replaced the natural community guided by mature females, with a male dominated society, an artificially created organisation.

The supreme aim of this society was to protect the gang of successful adolescents against revolutions or rebellions by other adolescent individuals or gangs.

With its culture, society tried to replace human community instinct with social consciousness. Dominated by the mind's selective awareness of reality, the adolescent mentality's culture did not succeed in replacing community instinct but simply confused or inhibited it.

Replacing the community with a society changed interpersonal relationships.

A community is above individual members because it represents their interdependence, their mutuality. A society instead is an association of independent and equal members which has to help them preserve their independence and equality.

A significant difference between a community and a society is that there is no social tension in the former. There is no social tension in a community because its members' individual differences are accepted as a natural part of life and as useful to the community. These differences inspire individuals' interdependence on which a community is built.

In a society, in which all individuals are considered equal, there is social tension. This tension is caused by the efforts, in the name of an abstract idea of equality, to ignore the physical and mental differences among individuals. This self-deception creates an emotional arousal which often errupts into discrimination or aggression.

Within a society, interpersonal relationships became a bargaining activity, a negotiated exchange of goods. Much of the social life of many people turned into a promotion or a sale of their main commodity: the self-created egos. A great deal of human life thus became a trade in fictional value or illusions. Everyone tried to realise an advantage or a profit at the expenses of others. This advantage or profit served the individual as evidence of the validity of his self-inflated ego. Even inborn self-preservation was replaced by the preservation of an imaginary ego. We also started practising suicide which mainly consisted of killing the despised self by an inflated ego.

The adolescent mentality's individual seldom realised the irony of his life. Whenever, in his interpersonal relationships, he obtained an undeserved advantage or profit, he developed a new fear, the fear of losing it, the fear of being outwitted or robbed of it. The psychosomatic arousal created by this fear was then used in the aggressive protection of undeserved advantage or profit.

It is interesting to note that political or religious revolutions only succeed when their leaders delegate part of their power to incompetent people, giving them positions which they do not deserve, jobs above their capabilities. The fear of losing a privileged position turns into a strong nervous energy which is then placed at the service of the ideologies and the leaders who gave them their unmerited advantages.

The best way to transform the adolescent mentality's society into a mature community, or a social life into communal life, would be to eliminate, with a sense of humour, our poses, roles, assumed masks, and to open ourselves to others, to expose our weaknesses and inferiorities. There is no community among equals or those pretending to be equal. Equals are not attracted to each other. A community is based on interpersonal attraction. There is no attraction without attractiveness and there is no attractiveness without openness or intimacy, both of which reveal the differences on which to build togetherness.

There is a big difference between the adolescent mentality's intimacy and the intimacy of maturity: the former means a bargaining intimacy, a negotiated denuding of two or more individuals in search of mutual exploitation. In fact, present day unhappiness, the increasing rate of suicides, mental disorders and psychosomatic diseases are mainly the result of a lack of real intimacy.

To really open oneself means to surrender one's self-created ego, but we only surrender our imaginary ego if we trust others. We do not trust others because we do not trust ourselves. We do not trust ourselves because we hide our genuine self behind a facade of artificial ego. In hiding we develop fear. In this fear we try to hide ourselves even more, to camouflage ourselves with decorations and poses.

By not hiding our real self behind the facade of our imaginary ego, we start trusting others. By opening ourselves to others we develop authentic intimacy with them. This is easily reached as openness is gentle, and gentleness disarms others' defences.

After all my efforts to show the negative side of the adolescent mentality's way of thinking and living, many people will claim that it is still a much more amusing and exciting way of life than the tranquillity and serenity of maturity. Many even search for ecstasy by living dangerously. I would like to stress that we have reached a point in which we can no longer be capricious or day-dream on a planet that could blow up at any moment. What is more, most of what we consider excitement today, boils down to tension or strain caused by emotional arousals, arousals created by fear in a life of day-dreams and illusions, of precariousness and precipices. Most of this tension and strain results in insomnia, agitation, cancer, psychosomatic diseases, mental disorders or suicide.

What is even more pathetic, is that we are guided or seduced by Utopian political ideologies or religious beliefs which are merely the results of the brain's constricted mental activity, operating under the pressure of high emotional arousals, originated by the fears of the mind's created precariousness and precipices. Exciting living is the product of a limited and irrational way of thinking.

Most interpersonal relationships consist of those between man and woman.

Ever since the adolescent revolution, man has tried to subjugate woman. Even in sexual relationships woman often has to please man, to follow his initiative, to accept his, often uncomfortable or humiliating sexual technique, which in many cases is merely a ritual of possession or domination.

The adolescent mentality male's hostility towards women must be mainly caused by his fear of their derision of his self-infatuation, or by his fear of their mockery of his masculinity and potency. One of the main derisions of a man's conceit was his woman's adultery. This is why for centuries woman's adultery was punished by death.

Fear of women is also evident in many men's interest in pornography. Confronted with the twisted, vulgar and undignified objectivisation of womens bodies, a man feels less challenged in his masculinity and potency.

In his emotional arousal, created by his fear of women, man not only fights and debases the female sex, but also fights the feminine traits he carries within himself. In fact, man only reaches maturity when he loses his aggressive masculinity, when he stops fighting the female part of himself.

In his division of labour man created feminine and masculine occupations, glorifying his own, and denigrating those of women.

Lately, however, changes are taking place in the structure of employment. Modern technology's elimination of hard work, in which man used to find his masculine identity has shaken his self-confidence. The manufacturing sector of the economy, once the monopoly and pride of 'Homo faber', has become manipulated by new electronic gadgets which women are as good at operating as men. The development of service industries and bureaucracy have also increased the number of working women.

The era of the sterotype sex-roles of the male bread-winner, and the female housekeeper is ending.

Professional ability, coupled with economic independence, have encouraged women to use their common sense, which is also shaking the main prejudices of the adolescent mentality.

Some of the so-called 'Womens Liberation Movements' do not contribute to this emancipation. On the contrary, certain women's main aim is to be the equal of adolescent men rather than to evolve into mature women. They fight to reach the adolescent mentality's achievements. Among these are: self-infatuation, ideological intoxication, life above one's means or merits, rhetoric, aggression, militancy, the 'après moi le déluge' attitude, psychosomatic diseases, mental disorders and laughableness. It is particularly ridiculous to see adult women thinking and behaving in the way, started thousands of years ago, by primitive teenagers.

Man often enters into marriage in order to assume the stereotype role of husband, a domineering patriarch, and to impose on his partner the stereotyped role of wife, an obedient domestic servant. This kind of marriage results in a game of roles. There can be no real intimacy in this game because roles lean on rules. To undress the body is not enough for intimacy. In order to reach a genuine intimacy, man must undress his mind of his prejudices; he should stop playing roles or assuming poses dictated by his conceited ego. A sense of humour helps. A sense of humour, in fact, can transform the marriage-game into an enjoyable marriage-play. Playing means sharing, and sharing is loving.

In marriage-play, husband and wife are seldom strangers to each

203

other. Play creates constant communication. Play also develops curiosity, mental alertness, progress in an experience in common, and above all, contact and interest in the playmate.

The marriage-game is a performance of two roles. A game of roles often brings boredom and boredom frightens the ego. Frightening people's egos, boredom either ends in a mania for sex or in divorce, and sometimes in both.

Marriage-play lasts longer than the marriage-game. The aim of a game is the fastest possible victory. The aim of play is to perpetuate itself.

We complain that marriage today is in a crisis. Marriage has been in a crisis even since it was invented. It was invented by man when he decided to replace the natural family created around the mother, with an artificial one created around the 'pater familias'. A real family cannot be built on an abstraction, an abstraction which has been forced onto the reality of life by legal coercion, physical force, threats and moral obligations. The patriarchal father's rights isolate him from his wife and children. In fact, the man dominated family lacks familiarity.

A genuine family is not based on a sense of possession or legal rules, but on a feeling of belonging.

We can all belong to a happy and big family, embracing the whole community, by behaving like a mature father, a motherly mother, a brotherly brother and a sisterly sister, a playful child, all according to the needs of others. That is why maturity's advice of 'know others' is more important than the adolescent mentality's 'know yourself.'

The role of man as a father is even more artificial and damaging to the familiarity of the family than that of a husband.

Children do not want a stereotyped patriarchal father. What they crave is a playmate. A father could transmit his experience and knowledge to his children much better by playing with them than by lecturing them. Through play, he could stimulate the optimal mental activity of their brains. Through play, a father could also establish intimate communication, lasting friendships and togetherness with his children, and vice-versa.

The role of the father usually intimidates children, thus perpetuating infancy. This inhibits the efficiency of the mothers' natural inclination: that of rearing infants to maturity.

Many adolescent mentality's fathers are self-centred. When a wife adapts herself to her husband's self-centredness, it is usually at the expense of her attention and dedication to her children. When the wife does not adapt herself to the self-centredness of her husband but to the care of her children, then the self-centred father may resent his children which transforms their lives into lives of fear and anxiety.

Man's organisation of marriage is ridiculous for one important reason. Unlike woman, man has no innate sense of organisation. A man's organisation is either inspired by abstract ideas, or is a cultural inheritance of the abstract ideas of the past. By its very nature, an organisation is concerned with the reality of the present and the future. Organisations inspired by abstract speculations, especially those belonging to the past, are neither realistic nor relevant.

In maturity a father becomes maternal, therefore co-operative. This implies sharing the task of rearing the children. This kind of family helps the children to widen their way of reasoning by liberating their minds from the rigidity and narrowness of contradictory opposites. With a wider reasoning, children realise that intelligent life does not consist of the precarious victories of one of the opponents, but of a continuum of consenses. Children must widen their way of reasoning because it is dangerous for life on our planet to manipulate more and more lethal weapons and progress in science and technology, with minds that have not advanced from the ancient immature phase of thinking.

Our present society has a system of education which prepares children for stereotyped roles in marriage. Boys are instructed to be masculine, assertive, competitive and aggressive; girls are told to be docile, feminine, submissive and obedient.

There is a problem some married couples face. If one of them has a strong adolescent mentality, the birth of a child can lead him or her to post-natal depression. This stressful state of existence is often caused by the idea that the baby means an end to the parent's free, selfish and self-centred life, and the start of a new responsibility.

Women with strong male adolescent mentalities dislike the feminine role and motherhood. Men with strong adolescent minds dislike the father's responsibility and maturity, as maturity implies maternity.

Another problem in marriage is what I would call chronic self-preciousness or callous coolness. This happens when one of the two, or both, think that they could have done better, that they could have found someone else, that his or her partner no longer appeals to his or her inflated ego, but they cannot divorce for moral, religious or financial reasons. Many children of such parents tend to find escape in various drugs when they reach adolescence.

A sense of humour could help solve these problems.

SEXUAL RELATIONSHIPS

Nowhere is the ridiculous side of the present adolescent mentality better illustrated than in its mania for sex and orgasm.

In the animal world so-called sexual arousal is mainly provoked by a biological discomfort. Why is a sexual arousal a biological discomfort?

One answer to this question may be the following. The growth of a living organism is an interplay between the biochemical potential of the original fertilised cell, and the external forces of the environment in which the interplay takes place. The climax of this interplay is when the organism stops its growth and reaches a relatively stable equilibrium with the external forces of its environment. We call this balanced result, maturity.

The end of this interplay, however, must leave certain marginal parts of the organism incomplete or undeveloped. These parts of the organism which are marginal, incomplete and unnecessary for the survival of the individual, may be what we call sex glands.

In its special seasonal optimal conditions, or under certain specific sensory or hormonal stimuli, the organism restarts its development and tries to expand beyond its balanced growth. This development mainly takes place through the marginal parts which were left undeveloped when the organism reached a balance in the interplay between its development potential and the external forces of its environment.

Perhaps because of the mature organism's established equilibrium with external forces, or perhaps due to their marginal and undeveloped nature, the sex glands, when activated, produce incomplete and undeveloped cells, which we call sex or germ cells, containing only half the chromosomes found in the normal cell of an organism.

Being incomplete and superfluous, the organism considers these sex cells foreign bodies, a nuisance causing a biological discomfort. What is more, in their virulence, these cells are irritating. It is in the nature of a living organism to eliminate its biological discomfort or to ease irritation. In fact, an organism mobilises it's defences to evacuate it's sex cells. The so-called reproductive glands of an organism, where the sex cells are produced, are usually placed in the proximity of organs specialised in the evacuation of the body's unnecessary fluids. Sex glands are, in fact, often served by these organs in the ejection of their secretion.

That sex cells are a biological imbalance and discomfort, can be seen in the malaise or distress of female animals when on heat. That the sex cells create a body's imbalance and discomfort, therefore certain specific fears, can be deduced by the fact that their excessive presence usually provokes the erection of the penis in male animals. In my view, it is not the activity of the testes which directly stimulates the penile erection, but that specific range of fears originated by the irritation that the virulent sex cells create. The erection of the penis is mainly ruled by the sympathetic system and endocrine glands related to it. These activities increase the blood flow to the erectile tissue of the penis. The activities of the sympathetic system and endocrine glands connected with it, are usually stimulated by fears caused by discomfort.

Many primates, and particularly when in captivity, get an erection when threatened.

The erection of penises in male fetuses, small boys and eunuchs can only be explained by an activity of the sympathetic system stimulated by some specific fears similar in their intensities to the fears of irritations created by the activity of the sex glands. In sleep, erection of the penis mainly takes place during the REM phases of sleep when the sympathetic system is active.

Fear of failing to perform well in competitive games, for example, can provoke clitoral and nipple erections in female athletes.

The energy necessary for the sexual activities of animals, is provided by the fears caused by the biological discomforts created by the superflous sex cells in their bodies. The emotional arousal caused by these fears is what we call sexual arousal

There is a specific range of fears, and therefore of activities of the sympathetic system and of the endocrine glands related to it, which cause penile and clitoral erections. Fears below this range do not produce these erections, while fears above this range usually concentrate the flow of blood towards the organs needed in an emergency, thereby limiting the flow of blood towards the erective tissues of the penis or clitoris.

That the presence in the body of sex cells is a physiological imbalance and discomfort can best be seen in the relief of an animal when it has discharged them through sexual intercourse. In my view, the main purpose of sexual intercourse in nature is not procreation, as is generally believed, but the elimination of the biological imbalance or discomfort created by the secretion of the sex glands in the body, to relieve an itch.

Fortunately for life, these incomplete male and female sex cells, when expelled and when meeting up in their affinity and complementarity, unite, forming a complete cell. In the right conditions this complete cell starts to produce a new organism. The meeting of the male and female sex cells is pure accident. There are no biological grounds for the theory that claims that the aim of all individuals in the living world is the perpetuation of the species. There is no such thing as a grand design or purpose in nature. The perpetuation, or disappearance of a species is accidental. As life itself is a cosmic accident, it is logical to assume that its perpetuation is a question of chance.

Many people claim that the reproduction of life is due to instinct. At the end of his life, Freud who gave prime importance to it finally admitted that it was a myth.

The superfluous sex cells produced by animals and plants in the optimal conditions are not only responsible for the reproduction of life, but also for its survival. Most food, such as eggs, fruit and cereal, are nothing but superfluous sex cells.

Other species must take us for insatiable sexual maniacs. No diurnal animal indulges in sexual intercourse at night, no nocturnal species in daylight, and none, with the exception of certain primates in captivity or on rare occasions, mate without the female seasonal sexual receptivity.

Why are we so obsessed with sex, persevering in this extra activity which is unnecessary for our survival, far beyond the needs of our species' reproduction, and which has now been proved to be the cause of cervical cancer and other diseases?

We have two kinds of sexual activity: the natural one inspired by the body's senses, and the unnatural one inspired by the mind. An obsession with sex is basically a disease of the mind. This obsession confuses our natural sexual drive.

Like any other greed or need of our ego, this obsession with sex is the result of precariousness and restlessness, created by emotional arousals, originated by our conceited and pretentious mind.

That this obsession with sex is a disorder of the mind can be deduced from the fact that we are the only species to indulge in sex with other animals, that we indulge in anal and oral intercourse, that we have invented all manners of sexual cruelty and perversion, and that we practise sexual abuse of children.

The hypothalamus plays a major role in the sexual activity of animals and humans. In animals, this role is mainly triggered by sensory or hormonal stimuli. In humans, it can also be manipulated by the mind.

The adolescent mentality male's ego feels the need to prove its validity with a success whenever it is shaken by reality. This frequently occurs in the over-pretentious. Sexual prowess tends to be the most appealing to an ego built around the idea of masculinity or virility. It is also one of the easiest to achieve as it is possible to develop sexual readiness purely by using our fantasies.

The body, however, has to provide extra energy for the sexual activity inspired by the needs of the mind. As I have stressed, the body mainly provides extra energy when frightened, and the mind supplies this fear whenever its world develops doubts, whenever its inflated ego is shaken. Most womanisers, from Casanova and

Don Juan, to modern sexual maniacs, are mainly insecure and fragile individuals in search of a boost to their egos. During revolutions or wars, when insecurity rules, sexual acitivity noticeably increases.

But what about the human female?

Conditioned by the adolescent mentality's culture, many females adapt themselves to man's world. They find their best method of survival in being, or pretending to be, what is expected of them. 'Man wants to be pleased in his ego, so let's please him,' is the motto of many women. It is the normal practice in many cases that, even in sexual intercourse, man does not try to satisfy his partner but only to fulfill his own ego. Often women guide men to reach satisfaction as quickly as possible, and are simply relieved when it is over. Some even fake orgasm in order to boost man's ego. In male dominated cultures, women provide services.

Where does a woman find the extra energy for her unnatural sexual activity?

Many women find this extra energy in the emotional arousal caused by a fear of not being seductive, of not being wanted, needed or desired, or in fear of loneliness and helplessness. Nymphomaniacs find the energy for their over-developed sex mania in their egos' exceptional fear of failure in their seductivity.

In the world of the adolescent mentality, most sexual intercourse, inspired by the mind, is the exploratory adventure of two self-loving people in search of exploitation, as only exploitation can satisfy pretentious egos. In most languages, in fact, sexual intercourse is described as 'making love'. After their mutually exploited togetherness, these two self-loving frightened and lonely people, however, often feel even more frightened and lonely.

Many people believe that our obsession with sex is inspired by the physical pleasure it gives. Freud went so far as to claim that the whole of life was ruled by this pleasure. He was partially right, but only the life of the adolescent mentality's humanity.

Inspired by inflated egos, our life consists mainly of the pursuit of achievements that please these egos. Pleasure in itself is a creation of the mind. It is triggered off by a satisfied ego, and consist of a drugged-like state due to the effect of natural opiates. Our opiates are secreted by our brain during the exertion we experience in our struggle for achievements, but their full effect only arrives when the ego has been appeased by a successful achievement, after the stress of the struggle is over. It seems that our natural opiates are not fully utilised or absorbed by the brain's receptors during an emotional arousal and its accompanying stress.

In the animal world, life is not the pursuit of pleasure, but the pursuit of the avoidance of pain, of the elimination of biological needs, of the riddance of physiological discomforts. Energy for these activities is provided for by the fears that biological pain, needs or discomforts carry.

After the elimination of its biological discomfort, an animal relaxes and reduces its activities to a minimum.

In satisfying their biological needs, many humans become restless. The reason for this is that the satisfaction of our needs pleases our ego, magnifying its importance and pretentiousness, which often increases our precariousness, therefore restlessness. This restlessness needs renewed achievements which can then please the increased infatuation of our egos. Such is the power of our mind that it can even transform the most strenuous activity into a pleasure, if it flatters our ego.

Most people choose to pursue those achievements which can best please his or her ego. Some may find satisfaction in intellectual achievements, some in those of the arts, some in those of a profession or trade, some in sport and some in material possessions or political power. In a society dominated by a culture which emphasises masculinity, male dominance and potency, a great number of men are obsessed with sexual achievements.

Perhaps it was this variety of pursuits of achievements that inspired Freud's theory of libido, and his theory of sublimation, a process by which a sexual energy was switched to some non-sexual activity. Freud would have done better had he placed libido inside the human mind and its conceited ego.

The role of the mind and its ego can even go so far as to damage the efficiency of the sexual glands. I have seen many professionally successful, self-confident and self-assertive men reach infertility. In my view, this is mainly due to the fact that the high emotional arousals, created by the fears that strong pretentiousness or over-ambition carry, which provide the extra energy for those people's aggression and self-assertion, noticeably depress the activitiy of the sexual glands. What is more, the low quantity of the sperm, produced during high emotional arousals, is less fertile, and less alive than average sperm. In fact, by being able to reduce people's pretentiousness or deride their over-ambition, a sense of humour and humour therapy could play a major role in curing infertility.

When the man has been offended in his masculinity and a woman in her feminity, in cultures where these are important, they can develop what could be called the mind's made castration, which is much deeper in its effect on sexual libido than a physical castration.

In the animal world sexual intercourse is a means of relieving the biological itch or discomfort caused by the irritation of virulent sex cells. Most animals deprived of their sex glands lose sexual interest.

In humans, sexual intercourse mainly serves as an instrument in achieving orgasm. Most humans, when deprived of their sexual glands, still carry on their sexual activity in search of orgasm.

What is an orgasm?

As I said, in a state of restlessness caused by the mind's created emotional arousal we develop the need for achievements. In their adolescent mentality, many people consider sexual success an impotant ego-booster. Through the mind's fantasies, the desire for sexual success creates sexual arousal.

We indulge, therefore, in a sexual relationship bearing two tensions: one caused by the mind's created emotional arousal, the other by the mind's instigated sexual arousal.

Tender physical contact, re-assuring cuddling and the gentle touching and caressing of the sensitive parts of the body during sexual play, coupled with loving, endearing and calming words, distract the mind's over-seriousness, the main source of emotional arousal. Cutting off the source of emotional arousal, the accumulated tension in the body erupts into an explosion, into massive spasmodic convulsions or contortions, which we call orgasm. The occurrence and intensity of an orgasm depends on the degree of the mind's abandonment and the amount of accumulated tension in the body. An orgasm seldom occurs if the mind is worried or over-serious. Frigidity and a strong mind go together.

One of the most powerful approaches to sexual play and one of the most successful shakers of the mind's over-seriousness is a sense of humour.

Some women find a closer intimacy and more calming caresses, therefore a more powerful orgasm, with other women. Some women are able to reach a more satisfying orgasm when they masturbate, than in sexual intercourse with a partner. In masturbation, these women feel more relaxed and freer in their sexual fantasies. The aim of these fantasies is to eliminate the mind's fears or worries. Some fantasise that they are being assaulted or raped, which helps them release their sense of responsibility or moral inhibitions. Some conceited women pretend that they are indulging in sexual intercourse with a popular actor or a famous pop singer; this flatters their minds, bringing them to relax.

When the sensitive parts of our body are caressed, gently massaged or kissed, our nervous system and body produce a special degree of emotional arousal which we translate into sexual excitement. Caressing, gentle massaging and kissing are all playful threats or mock attacks, which produce a range of special fears, a range of quasi fearless fears. The most erogenous parts of the body of an individual are usually also the most sensitive to real physical attacks.

Orgasm and laughter have much in common. They are both a discharge of the accumulated tension in a body o after the source of emotional arousals has been cut off, in orgasm by a re-assuring physical contact, cuddle or caress, in laughter by the derision or failure of the mind's expectations or pretentiousness.

Orgasm differs from laughter, however, in the sense that it takes longer to occur. While laughter is a sudden and immediate reaction, an orgasm usually needs a certain time to materialise. Perhaps this is due to the fact that during sexual play man's ego develops fear to not be able to be successful in his sexual performance, and woman's mind becomes frightened to relax, to abandon itself, or to leave its precious ego. It must be these fears which cause a strong increase in blood pressure, heart and the respiratory rates, lamentations, cries and agonized facial expressions, all of which reflect an internal struggle.

The external signs of laughter and orgasm are similar to those of epilepsy. Epileptic fits, in fact, are another form of liberation or discharge of the accumulated tension after the mind has been cut off by either a powerful fear, or by certain brain defects.

The male orgasm and seminal ejaculation usually coincide, but they are different in nature. The seminal ejaculation usually coincides with orgasm for the following reason: an orgasm is the end of the predominant role of the sympathetic nervous system. Only then can the activity of the parasympathetic nervous system, which controls the evacuation from the body of the superfluous fluids, be revived.

Small amounts of alcohol and mild tranquilizers facilitate achieving an orgasm as they help to reduce the mind's over-seriousness and worries. Increasing fears, however, large doses of alcohol and 'major' tranquilizers inhibit orgasm. Living in a state of strong fears, drug-addicts and people suffering from depression seldom reach orgasm.

Aphrodisiacs can help orgasm. To those who believe in them they are placebos, pleasing drugs, which placate the mind's worries and fears.

Orgasm is often followed by a period of twenty to forty minutes of catatonia, inertia or half consciousness. This drugged-like state of existence is caused by the effect of the brain's opiates, whose secretion was originated by the fears and worries which precede the orgasm, and which become fully active after the orgasmic climax, after the cessation of the predominant role of the sympathetic nervous system. These opiates operate on the limbic system, the emotional centre of the brain. During their effect, stimulation seldom provokes emotion.

Hyperventilation, or the excessive rate and depth of respiration which precedes and accompanies an orgasm, contributes to the post orgasmic semi-conscious state. This hyperventilation leads to a loss of carbon dioxide in the blood, which creates a form of anaesthesia, a sensation of lightness, floating or flying.

After the effects of the brain's opiates have disappeared, many people experience a melancholia, frightening emptiness or what could be called a 'success depression'. This depression is a result of the sensation of precariousness and loneliness created by an increase in the ego's conceit due to the success.

There are some forms of orgasm which are not the result of sexual intercourse. It is possible to experience a form of orgasm suddenly passing from a deep fear and stressful tension into safety and total relaxation after escaping peril or a failure of ego.

After scoring a goal, for example, a footballer and his team mates release their tension in orgasmic screams and manifestations. This orgasmic experience is followed by a short relaxed state, due to the effect of the players' naturally secreted opiates, a period in which the team is vulnerable to the opponents scoring.

Scientists and artists can experience what could be called 'eureka-orgasm'. An artist or a scientist can develop an intense desire to materialise an idea, but with this desire comes a fear of failing to realise it. In this fear an artist finds his creative energy and a scientist his energy for research. Eliminating this fear with his success an artist and a scientist can go through an orgasmic experience which is followed by the post orgasmic sensation of beatitude due to the brain's secreted opiates. When the effect of these opiates has disappeared, many artists and scientists develop a feeling of emptiness or a 'success depression'.

Love between man and woman with the adolescent mentality is created and governed by the needs of their respective minds, by the necessities of their infalted egos, ideal love being made by the idealised ego. Each idealised ego carries its ideal model of its particular love in its mind.

Man is attracted by a woman who flatters his sense of self-impotance, who can please his idea of masculinity, who can increase his feeling of potency, or who contributes to his fame or reputation. A female is attracted by a male who can please her socially and culturally conditioned ego. In the precarious world of the adolescent mentality, a woman's ego is often flattered by being desired by a man who can provide comfort, security and protection, all of which give her a sense of tranquility, and all of which, at the same time, boost the ego of the provider.

The union between man and woman established by this bargaining love, in which cheating and misunderstanding often take place, is a union of two alienated and lonely people in a world of alienation and loneliness. Being mainly a bargaining in illusions, this union often perpetuates alienation and loneliness.

The perpetuation of isolation and loneliness within a marriage or union, perpetuates selfishness, self-centredness, self-love and insensitivity, all of which are created by the emotional arousals produced by the fears that loneliness carries with it.

As adolescent mentality people are obsessed with sex, their love becomes intimately connected with it. In fact, many consider that a satisfactory marriage or relationship can only be realised and kept alive with a successful sexual relationship, implying a successful orgasm. Reaching orgasm together is the main aspiration of many husbands and wives, or people living together.

Among best sellers, there are many books dealing with the technique, explaining how to achieve a successful sexual performance and above all how to simultaneously reach an orgasm. Social workers spend much of their time trying to teach husbands and wives the art of sexual success, in their effort to save marriages that are on the rocks.

It is rather pathetic to learn that men and women in the adolescent mentality are seldom able to establish any other relationship or union but that which is based on sex. Freud went so far as to claim that any other relationship based on a noble friendship or a mutual understanding, respect or real love between men and women was nothing but a sublimation of their sexual instincts.

In adolescent love based on bargaining, sex becomes the main commodity.

Considering sex a commodity, we develop the strong desire of becoming the sole owner of the one we fancy. This possessiveness develops jealousy.

In this age of compulsive consumption, the sex commodity is

avidly devoured.

The adolescent mentality's form of love is a relatively recent acquisition of humanity, and thrives particularly in the Western World. It started with the cult of individual independence and the development of inflated egos. In the ancient world, our present form of love, and above all passionate love between man and woman, did not exist. Even today, in China and India, where the community and the family are still able to control individual independence and an individual's self-infatuation, our form of love is seldom practised.

The energy that adolescent love needs is provided for by the fear we develop when we meet our ideal, the fear of being unable to conquer him or her, or to lose him or her after a successful seduction.

That behind adolescent love lies fear can be deduced from the fact that being in love is an emotional arousal. In the emotional arousal created by being in love, like in any other emotional arousal, we experience high blood pressure, increase in heart beats and respiration rate, a reduced defficiency of our senses and perception, and a restricted mental activity.

In the adolescent mentality's love we can see how the same amount of hormones in the body, and the same activity of the sympathetic nervous system, can provoke both excitement and anxiety, ecstasy and agony, love and hate, all depending on how our ego responds to the emotional arousal caused by the fear that love carries.

The absence of a loved one can increase the fear of losing him or her, for ever, which increases insomnia, jealousy, palpitations, insecurity and irritability, and which brings a further reduced efficiency of the senses and perception, and an even more restricted mental activity. This is when the love can become a serious mental disorder. The more frightened we are of losing a loved one, the more passionate our love gets, the deeper our mental disorder becomes.

The reappearance or return of the loved one can provoke a state of delight due to the effect of the natural opiates secreted during the suffering, but which become effective after the suffering and stress disappear.

Losing the loved one irreparably can offend our ego to the point of creating excessive emotional arousals in which we can reach total insensitiveness and imperceptivity, coupled with an extremely restricted mental activity. The stress created by these excessive emotional arousals, produced by the loss of a loved one, can cause certain serious psychosomatic diseases or cancer.

Over-stimulating the hypothalamus, these excessive sufferings can noticeably distort the normal functioning of the appetite's centre, provoking a lack of interest in food in some, and over-eating in others. Those who find comfort in over-eating turn mainly to sweet things, probably because they remind them of their childhood. In suffering we all tend to resort to infancy.

Perhaps, because an adolescent's love is intimately connected with fear, suffering or stress, many languages use the expression 'to fall in love'.

One of the main aims of man in the adolescent mentality is paternal love, another invention of the adolescent mind. Paternal love means loving those who consider us omnipotent, who believe that we are unique, who admire or worship us.

By rewarding unconditional submission and obedience, and by punishing rebellion or disobedience, the aim of paternal love is to keep the loved ones in infancy, to stop the loved ones from growing up and maturing.

Paternal love reaches its apotheosis in the love of God.

Real love can only be felt with maturity. In maturity, men and women develop motherly love.

What is this motherly love?

It is a productive activity aimed at guiding infancy and adolescence to reach maturity. Contrary to paternal love which aims at keeping the loved ones in infancy, motherly love tries to help the helpless, to guide the lost, assist the needy, and to protect or encourage the frightened, all in order to bring them to maturity. For motherly love anyone who is helpless, lost, needy or frightened is an infant longing for assistance.

Brotherly or sisterly love can be of an adolescent or mature nature, depending on its selfishness or selflessness.

In a world dominated by the adolescent mentality, the majority of people never reach maturity. Many mothers never develop motherly love, merely loving their own children with a bargaining or calculating adolescent love.

What provides motherly love with the energy for its productive activity and concern, for its giving, caring and helping?

When we reach maturity with its serenity, we develop love of life; the whole life around us becomes a physical part of us. Another person or animal's pain becomes ours, fear felt by others becomes our fear, and the discomfort of others becomes ours. It is in the emotional arousals caused by the pain, fear or discomfort in others that a mature person finds his or her energy for motherly love. In its intuitive realisation, maturity considers that life is interrelated, and that an individual's serenity can only be achieved and preserved in surrounding serenity.

A mature person reaches an optimal sensitiveness, perception and mental activity which enables him or her to participate fully in the totality of life. That is why motherly love senses the smallest sign of someone in need and the slightest sound of the frightened.

It is said that giving is receiving. This is indeed true. Giving reduces or eliminates the fears of those in need. With the reduction or elimination of their fears, they also reduce or eliminate their emotional arousals, tension and stress, thereby reducing or eliminating their selfishness, self-centredness, self-love or their panicky way of thinking and behaving. All this broadens their sensitiveness, perception and their way of reasoning, developing understanding and concern for others, in other words, their motherly love. Giving helps those who receive to mature and become productive and fruitful.

Selfishness, self-centredness, self-love and a restricted way of thinking are caused by high emotional arousals, mainly originated by the mind's self-made fears. These fears can be driven away by the elimination of the mind's pretentiousness and conceit. A sense of humour helps to shake these fantasies, and reduce our inflated ego to the level of our true self.

Bringing us back from illusions to reality, a sense of humour enables us to realise that we can only reach contentment in a contented environment. With a sense of humour reasoning we find that the unhappiness and gloom of others is infectuous. That is why the pursuit of personal happiness only acquires a realistic meaning if it becomes the pursuit of other people's happiness. This may sound naive to those with a restricted and immature logic and reasoning.